D0795153

MANAGING SCARCITY

STATE OF HEALTH SERIES

Edited by Chris Ham, Director of Health Services Management Centre, University of Birmingham

MANAGING SCARCITY

Priority Setting and Rationing in the National Health Service

Rudolf Klein, Patricia Day and Sharon Redmayne

Open University Press
Buckingham · Philadelphia

Open University Press
Celtic Court
22 Ballmoor
Buckingham
MK18 1XW

Learning Resources
Centre
1 2089737

and
1900 Frost Road, Suite 101
Bristol, PA 19007, USA

First Published 1996

Copyright © Rudolf Klein, Patricia Day and Sharon Redmayne 1996

All rights reserved. Except for the quotation of short passages for the purpose of criticism and review, no part of this publication may be reproduced, stored in a retrieval system, or transmitted, in any form or by any means, electronic, mechanical, photocopying, recording or otherwise, without the prior written permission of the publisher or a licence from the Copyright Licensing Agency Limited. Details of such licences (for reprographic reproduction) may be obtained from the Copyright Licensing Agency Ltd of 90 Tottenham Court Road, London, W1P 9HE.

A catalogue record of this book is available from the British Library

ISBN 0 335 19447 8 (hb)   0 335 19446 X (pb)

Library of Congress Cataloging-in-Publication Data

Klein, Rudolf, 1930–
     Managing scarcity : priority setting and rationing in the National
Health Service / Rudolf Klein, Patricia Day, and Sharon Redmayne.
          p.   cm. — (The State of health)
     Includes bibliographical references and index.
     ISBN 0-335-19447-8 (hb)   0 335 19446 X (pb)
     1. National Health Service (Great Britain)   I. Day, Patricia.   II.
Redmayne, Sharon, 1964–   .   III. Title.   IV. Series.
RA412.5.G7K54   1996
362.1'0941—dc20   96-18743
                                                                      CIP

Typeset by Type Study, Scarborough, North Yorkshire
Printed in Great Britain by St Edmundsbury Press,
Bury St Edmunds, Suffolk

CONTENTS

SERIES EDITOR'S INTRODUCTION

Health services in many developed countries have come under critical scrutiny in recent years. In part this is because of increasing expenditure, much of it funded from public sources, and the pressure this has put on governments seeking to control public spending. Also important has been the perception that resources allocated to health services are not always deployed in an optimal fashion. Thus at a time when the scope for increasing expenditure is extremely limited, there is a need to search for ways of using existing budgets more efficiently. A further concern has been the desire to ensure access to health care of various groups on an equitable basis. In some countries this has been linked to a wish to enhance patient choice and to make service providers more responsive to patients as 'consumers'.

Underlying these specific concerns are a number of more fundamental developments which have a significant bearing on the performance of health services. Three are worth highlighting. First, there are demographic changes, including the ageing population and the decline in the proportion of the population of working age. These changes will both increase the demand for health care and at the same time limit the ability of health services to respond to this demand.

Second, advances in medical science will also give rise to new demands within the health services. These advances cover a range of possibilities, including innovations in surgery, drug therapy, screening and diagnosis. The pace of innovation is likely to quicken as the end of the century approaches, with significant implications for the funding and provision of services.

Third, public expectations of health services are rising as those who use services demand higher standards of care. In part, this is stimulated by developments within the health service, including the availability of new technology. More fundamentally, it stems from the emergence of a more educated and informed population, in which people are accustomed to being treated as consumers rather than patients.

Against this background, policymakers in a number of countries are reviewing the future of health services. Those countries which have traditionally relied on a market in health care are making greater use of regulation and planning. Equally, those countries which have traditionally relied on regulation and planning are moving towards a more competitive approach. In no country is there complete satisfaction with existing methods of financing and delivery, and everywhere there is a search for new policy instruments.

The aim of this series is to contribute to debate about the future of health services through an analysis of major issues in health policy. These issues have been chosen because they are both of current interest and of enduring importance. The series is intended to be accessible to students and informed lay readers as well as to specialists working in this field. The aim is to go beyond a textbook approach to health policy analysis and to encourage authors to move debate about their issue forward. In this sense, each book presents a summary of current research and thinking, and an exploration of future policy directions.

Professor Chris Ham
Director of Health Services Management Centre
University of Birmingham

INTRODUCTION

This is a book about 'rationing', in its widest sense, in Britain's National Health Service: from Cabinet decisions about how much money to allocate to the NHS in its annual public expenditure review, through decisions by health authorities about how to allocate their budgets, to decisions by individual clinicians about who should get treated, when and how. It is clinicians who take the final rationing decisions, when they decide which patients should go to the head of the queue, what kind of interventions should be carried out and, in rare cases, who should be denied treatment. But they do so within the constraints set by a series of decisions about the resources that should be made available, and how these resources should be distributed to different parts of the country and to different sectors of health care, cascading down from central government.

The aim of this book is to analyse this process. But although the focus is on Britain's NHS, the issues raised are wider. All health care systems ration the availability of, or access to, services, if in different ways. Nor is rationing simply a function of the amount of resources a country devotes to health care. American scholars were among the first to draw attention to the issue of rationing (Fuchs 1974; Mechanic 1979), despite the fact that the proportion of the national income devoted to health care in the United States is twice that of Britain. Everywhere, indeed, there appears to be a growing gap between supply and demand, reflecting both demography and the seemingly limitless opportunities for medical intervention created by technology (de Kervasdoué *et al.* 1984). There is scarcity even among plenty; spending more does not seem to diminish worry (Wildavsky 1975).

To investigate rationing is therefore to examine the different strategies available and adopted to manage scarcity. Nor is health care unique in this respect. The same dilemmas, the same necessity to make choices, the same need to cope with the gap between supply and demand are evident in all welfare services and programmes where neither the total budget nor its allocation to individuals is determined by the market. Britain's NHS is, in this respect, a case study of a more general phenomenon. Studying it allows us to draw some conclusions applicable to the whole field of social policy. First, it illuminates the respective roles of politicians, professionals and other actors in the process by which national decisions about the level of collective provision are translated into individual decisions about who gets what. Second, it allows us to examine the kind of strategies adopted, and the kind of arguments involved, in allo- cating scarce resources: how fairness and justice are defined in practice.

The first part of the book concentrates on rationing as a general phenomenon. It starts by trying to unpackage the notion of ration- ing. Can rationing, a highly emotive concept calculated to raise the temperature of any debate in which it is invoked, be distinguished from priority-setting, a more neutral term? It then examines those issues, like the debate about the principles that should determine the allocation of scarce resources, which cut across services and programmes. In doing so, it illustrates the arguments by looking at practice in a variety of social policy fields. This provides the context, and the intellectual framework, for the second part, which exam- ines policy and practice in the NHS and how these have changed since the 1991 reforms of the service. In the third part, we review the different strategies that are available, drawing on the experience of both Britain and of other countries.

This book has its origins, and foundations, in a study of priority- setting and rationing in the NHS funded by the Nuffield Provincial Hospitals Trust and the National Association of Health Authorities and Trusts. This involved analysing the purchasing plans published by health authorities in England from 1992 to 1995 and carrying out ten case studies of decision-making in individual health authorities. The case studies were chosen to represent a wide range of situ- ations: the health authorities concerned ranged from hard pressed inner-city purchasers faced with budget cuts to non-metropolitan ones which serenely looked forward to a rising income. The former exercise was designed to provide an overall picture of the priorities being set by health authorities and how these changed over time. The latter, involving interviews with decision-makers in individual health authorities, was designed to examine the process of decision-making and the kind of factors that shaped (and constrained) the decisions made. Throughout our focus is exclusively on the health authorities who, between them, control over 80 per cent of the NHS's budgets. Although general practitioner fundholding is growing in scale and scope, virtually nothing is known about how they allocate their resources; another study would be needed.

In addition, we have drawn selectively on the rapidly growing international academic literature on the ethics, economics and practice of rationing, both in health care and in other fields. Even so, we have discovered that there are still vast regions of the intellectual map where we are in the position of the early geographers who marked unexplored tracts of country 'here be dragons'. In this particular instance, the dragons are the professionals actually delivering services: we know remarkably little about how doctors make their allocative decisions. However, only by exploring the wider context and trawling the international literature is it feasible to identify what is special to the NHS (if anything) and what is common to all systems that distribute resources according to non-market criteria. And unless we can 'place' the NHS within such a wider context, it is impossible to contribute to the wider international debate about rationing: the hope of this book.

We have written this book with the help and cooperation of a large number of people in the NHS: health authority managers, non-executive directors and doctors. There are too many to thank by name even if we had not done our interviewing on the basis of non-attributability in order to ensure maximum frankness. All we can do, therefore, is to express our gratitude in general terms. In one case, however, we can break our anonymity rule: we would like to thank Mrs Thelma Brown, who organized us and our work during the research project which generated the raw material, as well as nursing us through the process of writing this book.

PART I

THE CONTEXT

1

UNPICKING THE NOTION

Rationing is a word whose semantic origins evoke the notion of reason but whose use often prompts unreason. If we consult the dictionary, we find that rationing is first cousin – grafted on to the same Latin root stock – to rationality. It conveys a sense of proportionality, of dividing scarce resources fairly, of ensuring that everyone gets his or her share. But in practice rationing is an emotion-laden word. Depending on the context in which it is used, and the kind of rationing that is involved, it may evoke either approval or anger. It is therefore a word which has to be used with some care. The purpose of this chapter is accordingly to unpick the notion, to distinguish the various dimensions of the concept and to develop a framework for analysing the different ways in which rationing may manifest itself. Indeed, we shall go on to argue that, in order to avoid confusion, the use of the word rationing should itself be strictly rationed. It should be reserved to describe the process by which resources are allocated to individuals at the point of service or programme delivery, while 'priority setting' should be used to describe the process of determining the budgets, and their distribution, which constrain the decisions about who gets what. Semantic pedantry will, in this case, help to clarify the argument.

The sensitivity to context of how rationing is perceived, and how its meaning is interpreted, is well illustrated by wartime Britain. In the war years rationing became a symbol of social solidarity and of a shared commitment to a national enterprise. 'People are willing to bear any sacrifice if a 100 per cent effort can be reached and the burden fairly borne by all', a 1942 Ministry of Information survey concluded (cited in Hennessy 1993). Rationing became a national institution. But the necessary condition for this acceptance of 'institutionalized privation', as Hennessy points out, was conspicuous fairness: the universalization of stringency. The black market was synonymous with crime and spivvery. In contrast, rationing in health care – and other social services – tends to attract attention, and to stir public emotions, when it concerns visible, identifiable individuals: when the burden of inadequacy is shared out in ways that appear arbitrary or discriminatory. In other words, and here we come back to the root of the word, the acceptability of rationing seems to depend on its perceived reasonableness, which, in turn, appears to depend on the form it takes.

Rationing can take many forms. There is rationing by price, i.e. allowing market power to determine who gets what. But even in circumstances when rationing by price is rejected as an allocative principle – as it is in the NHS and the other public services and programmes which are discussed in this book – it can take many forms. In the attempt to develop an understanding of rationing, it is therefore helpful to make two distinctions as a first step. First, rationing may be universal or selective. That is, it may affect the population as a whole, as in the case of wartime Britain, or specific groups within it. If it involves specific groups – such as social services for the elderly or those out of work – then the process may be particularly sensitive to challenges about arbitrary, discretionary decisions in the allocation of resources. And the sensitivity may be all the greater if such selective, group-specific services or programmes are provided in parallel with market provision; if, in short, some people have the resources needed to buy themselves out of the rationing process. The specific form that such selective rationing takes – discussed below – may thus be crucial.

Second, rationing may take place at different levels. It may involve decisions either about setting budgets (macro rationing or, more accurately, priority setting) for specific services and programmes, and about the distribution of resources within them, or about how to allocate those resources to individuals using those services (micro rationing). The level of decision-making will, in turn, determine the kind of criteria used and the actors involved in the process. In what follows we therefore set out the different levels of the rationing process, before turning to the different forms that rationing may take. Subsequent chapters will then examine the actors involved at each level and address the question of the different criteria that may be invoked.

PRIORITY SETTING AND RATIONING

A simple proposition shapes the analysis of this book. This is that rationing, in the wide sense of decisions about the allocation of scarce resources, takes place in circumstances when supply is constrained by considerations of cost but demand is not restrained by considerations of price. Thus defined, rationing is a characteristic of all those publicly provided or funded services and programmes – like the NHS, social services, housing, education and some parts of social security – where constrained budgets meet unconstrained demands for resources. And it follows that the first level of rationing is national: decisions about the budgets for particular services and programmes are taken as part of that great British autumn ritual, the Cabinet's public expenditure review. It is this round of ministerial wrangling, with the Treasury lined up against spending departments, which determines the financial envelopes within which services and programmes operate.

In ordinary usage this process is not described as rationing but as priority setting: it involves ministers deciding on their priorities not only between different programmes but also between spending more and cutting taxes or reducing the public borrowing requirement. In what follows, we shall adopt this usage in line with the definitional distinction made earlier, while noting that it is these macro decisions which determine the constraints within which micro decisions about the allocation of resources to individual beneficiaries of the programmes are taken.

The next level is when the local authorities or the agencies of central government responsible for delivering services or programmes decide on their priorities. Their ability to vary national priorities depends on a number of factors, constitutional and practical. Local authorities have most freedom, although it has been greatly reduced in recent years (Jenkins, 1995a). So, for example, if central government reduces expenditure on education, local authorities can – notionally at least – maintain their spending by cutting back elsewhere. In contrast, health authorities have considerably less freedom, in theory at least, since they are agents of central government – though in practice, as we shall see in Chapters 4 and 5, the picture is rather more complicated. Social security offices have least freedom. Like health authorities, they are agents of central government without any independent source of finance. Additionally, however, the distribution of their funds is determined by nationally fixed entitlements. Only in the case of payments from the budget-capped Social Fund (see Chapter 2) have local offices any discretion in the allocation of resources.

The last point illustrates a more general proposition. The scope for discretion in the manipulation of national priorities at the second level of decision-making varies with the specificity of the decisions taken by central government. To the extent that central government determines not only the total funding allocation but also its distribution within budgetary envelopes – whether to client groups or to specific services (e.g. nursery schools within the education budget or spending directed to dealing with AIDS within the NHS budget) – so it limits the ability of subordinate agencies to set their own priorities and moves nearer to the front line of rationing in the strict sense: the distribution of resources by service deliverers.

The third level is at the point of service delivery, where those responsible for providing services or making payments decide on who is to get what within the budgetary limits that they have been set. It is at this point in the hierarchy of decision-making that doctors decide on which patients to treat, social workers decide on the eligibility of clients for residential care and housing officers decide to whom to allocate homes. This is rationing in the strict sense.

This schematic way of presenting the decision-making hierarchy is, clearly, over-simple (Glennerster 1975). There are some kinds of decisions that cut across the levels (Harrison and Hunter 1994). Either central government or some of the second-level authorities and agencies may specify the conditions governing the distribution of resources. That is, they may define the criteria for resource allocation at the point of distribution either by specifying entitlements (e.g. to old age pensions or unemployment benefit) or by setting out rules for determining eligibility (e.g. that social housing should be reserved for the homeless or other particularly disadvantaged groups). This is what might be called categorical rationing. Finally, of course, the first two levels may decide to limit what is on offer by limiting the scope of the services and programmes concerned: rationing by exclusion. In doing so, they limit – although, as we shall see, they do not necessarily eliminate – the discretion of those operating at the third level. Rationing, in short, can take many forms – at different levels – and in the next section we elaborate this point.

FORMS OF RATIONING

Strategies for coping with demands under the constraints of budget limits, by limiting the resources going to any one individual, can take many forms (Judge 1978; Scrivens 1979). Building on Parker (1975), we can distinguish between at least seven forms of rationing: by denial, by selection, by deflection, by deterrence, by delay, by dilution and by termination. In the following list we elaborate on each of these in turn.

- *Rationing by denial.* This is the most brutal (and visible) form of rationing. Would-be beneficiaries of services or programmes are turned away, on the grounds that they are not suitable or that their needs are not urgent enough. In effect, the threshold of eligibility for a particular service is raised or lowered in order to match supply and demand. Conversely, the functions of a particular programme or service are redefined to exclude specific types of clients or forms of intervention.
- *Rationing by selection.* This is the converse of rationing by denial but can have the same outcome. Service providers select those clients or would be beneficiaries who are most likely to benefit from intervention (and will therefore improve the success rate of the programme concerned), are seen as deserving cases or are least likely to cause any problems.
- *Rationing by deflection.* Instead of being turned down flat, would-be beneficiaries are steered towards another programme or service. In effect, agencies safeguard their own resources by dumping the problem in the lap of someone else. An education problem becomes redefined as a social services problem; a social services problem becomes redefined as a housing problem; a housing problem becomes redefined as a social security problem, and so *da capo*.
- *Rationing by deterrence.* Instead of an outright denial of access, it can simply be made more difficult. There is a large repertory of mechanisms for doing so, all of which are apt to discourage use by raising barriers to, and the costs of, entry into the system. Telephonists may be unhelpful; receptionists may be chillingly dismissive; information leaflets may be unavailable; forms may be incomprehensible; there may be long queues of people waiting for attention in dismal surroundings.
- *Rationing by delay.* Once the barriers have been overcome, once access to the system has been achieved, there still remain other

options for discouraging demand. Appointments may be made for weeks or months ahead; an exchange of letters may be turned into a test of endurance; finally, there is the ultimate symbol of rationing by delay, the waiting list.

● *Rationing by dilution*. If demand cannot be reduced sufficiently by the use of all these strategies, there remains the dilution option. Services or benefits are indeed offered, but their scale and 'depth' are reduced. No one is excluded but everyone gets less. Social workers visit their clients less often; doctors order fewer tests; teachers spend less time with each child. If quantity cannot be cut, quality may be reduced.

● *Rationing by termination*. The repertory of rationing strategies is still not exhausted by the above list. There remains the last option: terminating treatment or intervention. The social worker can declare a case closed; doctors can discharge patients; the difficult child can be expelled from the school.

These strategies are not exclusive. All or some can be deployed in combination. Nor need they necessarily be conscious or deliberate rationing devices: they may simply represent the way in which those concerned with service or programme delivery make life more tolerable for themselves when they are under budgetary and other pressures. And they will inevitably be used in different ways in different services and programmes, depending on the nature of the 'goods' being delivered. In the next chapter we examine the way in which the 'goods' being delivered differ and how rationing takes place in specific services and programmes.

2

POLITICS AND STRATEGIES

Even though both priority setting and rationing are near-universal phenomena in all services or programmes with closed budgets and open-ended demands, it does not follow that the form they take will necessarily be the same. Given that there are such a wide variety of rationing strategies, as we saw in the previous chapter, it may be that the choice among them is dependent on the characteristics of the policy field. The first section of this chapter seeks to identify the factors that could be thought to influence, in theory at least, the strategies adopted in different policy environments. The second section analyses practices in a number of settings to test whether there are, indeed, differences in the rationing strategies adopted. In this, the aim is to provide some benchmarks against which it will be possible subsequently to judge the extent to which rationing strategies are contingent on specific circumstances and whether health care – the main subject of this study – is a special case or can be treated as an example of a more general pattern.

As a first step, consider the actors involved in decision-making at the three levels identified in Chapter 1. At the national level, the key decision makers are the Cabinet ministers and civil servants involved in determining the relative priority to be given to different spending programmes. At the next, or middle, level it is councillors and their officials in the case of local authority services and, in the case of the NHS, members of health authorities – a mixture of managers and nominated non-executives – who make the allocative decisions. At the third, or micro, level, it is those responsible for service or programme delivery working within their set budgets.

This suggests that, as far as the first two levels are concerned, there is much commonality across services such as education, housing and social services among the actors involved. The lead actors are politicians, whether local or national, with officials in a supporting role. However, the middle level of the NHS is different from the other services concerned in one crucial respect. Here the lead actors lack any kind of independent constituency or political legitimacy. In the case of the NHS, health authorities are – in the words of its founder, Nye Bevan – the 'creatures' of the minister. Their accountability, in the strong sense of having to answer for their jobs if their performance fails to satisfy (Day and Klein 1987), is to the centre. Similarly, in the case of social security, the regional level is administrative only. In these two instances we might therefore expect, in theory, that there is less discretion in the choice of rationing strategies at the middle level.

It is when we move to the third level, the point of service or programme delivery, that we find most diversity, however. To the extent that the choice and use of rationing strategies involve discretion in the allocation of resources, so we might expect this to vary with the characteristics of the front-line personnel. Specifically, it might be expected to vary with the status of those delivering services: the extent to which they can claim professional status and, what goes with such status, autonomy in the exercise of their craft. Thus doctors, as members of a high-status profession with a monopoly of esoteric knowledge and expertise (Freidson 1971), claim autonomy in the way they use their clinical judgement in the allocation of resources to individual patients. The professional status of social workers and teachers is, in contrast, less secure and their control over the use of resources might accordingly be expected to be more circumscribed. Finally, when we move to housing or social security, those involved in service delivery tend to be officials without any claim to professional status. They are administrators whose discretion is fettered by rules: they supposedly implement decisions made at higher levels in the hierarchy of policy-making.

Before we see whether these *a priori* assumptions are borne out by practice – which we do in the second half of this chapter – there is a further factor to be considered. This is the nature of the 'goods' being allocated. The goods may vary on a number of dimensions: their divisibility, their substitutability and their visibility. The terms are largely self-explanatory. Divisibility refers to the extent to which it is possible to stretch resources by delivering smaller packages of the goods in question. Substitutability refers to the extent to which it is possible to replace an expensive service by a cheaper one. Visibility refers to the extent to which rationing is perceived to be the result of decisions about the allocation of resources, as distinct from decisions taken as a result of following professional judgement or administrative rules.

So, for example, money is highly divisible. It might therefore be expected that dilution rather than denial strategies – limiting the amounts of individual benefits rather than turning people away – might be followed in the case of social security officials administering the budget-capped Social Fund. Similarly, the time of teachers and social workers is highly divisible. Again, therefore, we might expect rationing to take the form of dilution rather than denial: teachers and social workers might simply spend less time with each pupil or client. Divisibility, in turn, tends to be associated with lack of visibility insofar as strategies of dilution are less dramatic than strategies of denial.

In contrast, health care and housing seem, at first sight at least, to score less highly on the divisibility dimension. A surgeon cannot stretch limited resources by carrying out half an operation; a housing officer cannot make a limited number of dwellings go further by allocating half a house. However, in both these instances, there may be scope for substitutability. Instead of an operation, a course of drugs may be prescribed. Instead of a house on a new estate, a flat in an unpopular tower block or a place in a hostel may be offered.

In the case of health care, in any case, there may be more scope for divisibility than the example of surgical operations suggests. Doctors and nurses can, like teachers and social workers, decide on how much time to spend on each patient. Rationing by dilution is therefore a viable option. Only in the case of allocative decisions where resource constraints are not the limiting factor – for example, where the supply of organs for transplants is limited – must rationing inescapably take the form of denial: some (possibly highly visible) patients must go without treatment.

There remain the various other strategies of rationing outlined in the previous chapter: by deflection, by deterrence and by termination. Such strategies would seem to be available, irrespective of the nature of the 'goods' being allocated by different services or programmes. They have the advantage – from the point of view of the service funders and deliverers – that they tend to lack visibility. They tend to affect all potential users of the services, in subtle and oblique ways, rather than pointing the searchlight of public attention on identifiable individuals. We might therefore expect them to be used irrespective of the nature of the 'goods' being delivered.

They invest the practice of rationing with a cloak of invisibility, so lessening its political costs.

The third section of this chapter examines resource allocation at the point of service delivery in a variety of services, using this framework in order to test the assumptions about the context-contingent nature of rationing. Before this, however, we examine the practice of priority setting at the national and intermediate levels.

PRIORITY SETTING IN PRACTICE

The framework for rationing in the public sector is set, as already noted, by the government's annual autumn statement (Chancellor of the Exchequer 1995), which sets out the expenditure plans for the coming years as part of its overall economic strategy. The expenditure plans themselves reflect the government's priorities as between spending on public services and programmes, on the one hand, and tax cutting and deficit reduction, on the other. It is these decisions which determine the overall level of spending. But within this overall level, choices then have to be made as to how to allocate the available resources between the competing claims of different departments and programmes. It is these choices which eventually determine the resources available at the point of service or programme delivery and define the nature of the rationing dilemma.

Consider, for example, the 1995 public expenditure plans. These provided for an increase in total spending of £6.5 billion as between 1995–6 and 1996–7: a rise of just over 2 per cent. But this was distributed, unsurprisingly and as always, unequally between different departments. The NHS got an extra £1.1 billion (3.3 per cent); schools got an extra £878 million (6.2 per cent); the Department of Social Security got an extra £3.1 billion (4.2 per cent). The problem about these figures is that it is extraordinarily difficult either to derive from them a coherent picture of the government's priorities or to assess their impact at the point of service delivery. The fact that a specific department or programme gets more than its share of the extra money available (or less than its share of pain if cuts are being made) does not necessarily mean that it is being accorded higher priority than its competitors or that its rationing dilemmas will be any less painful.

For although the figures may be highly visible, their meaning is often opaque. They tell us nothing about the relationship between spending levels and changes in the demand for the services or programmes concerned (the result of demographic, economic and social trends) or about the scope for using existing resources more efficiently. Their significance, moreover, is contingent on the rate of change in the level of salaries and wages in different services or programmes: an apparent increase in the budget may be mopped up by salary settlements that leave no scope for funding growth in service provision. Only in the case of programmes of categorical entitlements such as social security benefits are the government's priorities clear cut and highly visible: so that it is possible to tell, for example, that ministers put higher priority on benefits for the elderly than on those for the young.

The significance of first-level or national decisions about priorities therefore tends to be that they are defined in political debate – and, though only posthumously, in academic analysis (see, for example, Hills 1990) – rather than speaking for themselves. The problem of interpreting expenditure decisions about the NHS is considered in more detail in the second part of this book. Here it is sufficient to note problems common to all services and programmes. Priorities are about the balance between supply and demand. If demand for a particular service or programme falls, then even a stable budget may indicate a high degree of priority. If demand rises, conversely, then even an increased budget may imply more stringent rationing at the point of delivery. The difficulty is to define both demand and supply (Klein, 1975). In some cases demand may be 'read off' demographic trends: if the number of children of school age rises, then it is self-evident that demand is rising. But in other cases, such as the social services or housing, the programmes themselves define the demand: this, indeed, is what rationing is all about. Supply may also be a problematic concept, if to a lesser extent than demand. Changes in financial budgets may not necessarily be an accurate indicator of the resources available for allocation. The costs of providing a particular service or programme may be rising faster than the general increases in prices, in which case a stable budget may indicate a cut in resource availability. Conversely, if costs are rising more slowly or if efficiency is improving, a stable budget may mean an increase in resource availability.

The analysis of national priorities is a somewhat arcane art form: the public's concern is not with statistics but with the impact on services and programmes. And since this is often difficult to discern, except retrospectively, the result is that the significance or meaning of the first-level decisions is largely determined by the reaction of those working at the third level. If those responsible for allocating resources to individuals respond to the government's decisions by denouncing the inadequacy of the budgets set, and if this interpretation carries conviction, then there is likely to be a general perception of inadequacy. The rationing strategies of those at the point of service delivery will thus be legitimated as the inevitable outcome of government policies. The micro implementation of national priorities will, in turn, shape the way in which the macro decisions are perceived. Rationing at the point of service delivery is thus not only the product of national decisions but also affects how those decisions are viewed. The relationship is a two-way rather than a hierarchic one.

Complicating the problem of interpreting national decisions about priorities is the scope for varying them at the second level. This is most apparent in the case of services run by local authorities. At this level national priorities are transmuted into local ones, so adding a further layer of complexity to the problem of interpreting the significance of national decisions. The variations in spending levels on particular services or programmes between local authorities are a much explored territory, so a few examples will suffice (Audit Commission 1995a). Consider the pattern of education spending in two counties: Humberside and Hertfordshire. The first spends just over £4000 a year on each secondary pupil in its schools but only £1400 on each child under five; the latter spends £2770 and £2047 respectively. So, clearly, they have contrasting priorities about the appropriate level of spending on different categories of children, with significant implications for those at the point of service delivery. A similar picture emerges when spending on social services is examined. Again, consider two counties: Staffordshire and Somerset. The first spends £60 per head of population on the care of elderly people and £3.82 on people with mental health problems. The second spends £44.50 and £5.50 respectively. Again, local priorities between groups competing for resources are very different – even allowing for the fact that some of the variations may be explained by demographic and other social factors – as are the implications for rationing at the point of service delivery. And, as we shall see, a similar picture emerges when we turn to the NHS in the second part of the book.

There is thus no necessary direct linkage between national decisions about priorities, once they have been filtered through the agencies and authorities at the second level, and rationing at the point of service delivery. It is only when central government itself sets the budgets of the responsible agencies – as in the first of our examples in the next section – that there would seem to be a direct link. But even in these cases, as we shall see, the scope for interpretative discretion remains large.

RATIONING IN PRACTICE: SOME CASE STUDIES

Our first case study is of rationing in the distribution of money, the most divisible of all goods. The Social Fund is designed to respond to the exceptional needs of people who are receiving social assistance benefits or who are dependent on low incomes. Since 1991 it has operated on a capped budget. The Department of Social Security allocates annual budgets to its local offices, and specialist officers in each decide who should be given how much by way of either discretionary grants or loans. It is local offices, in other words, that have to balance the supply of money and demand from applicants over the financial year. In what follows we describe how this balance is achieved, drawing on a study carried out by the Social Policy Research Unit at the University of York (Huby and Dix 1992; Walker *et al.* 1992).

The 1988 Directions issued by the Secretary of State for Social Security defined the eligible groups and provided guidance about the needs that *could* be met by Social Fund payments. First, there are budgeting loans, designed to help people 'to meet important intermittent expenses' for which it may be difficult to budget. Second, there are crisis loans; so, for example, payments may be made to meet expenses in an emergency provided that 'the provision of such assistance is the only means by which serious damage or serious risk to the health or safety of that person, or a member of his family, may be prevented'. Third, there are community care grants, designed to help someone 'to re-establish himself in the community following a stay in institutional or residential care' or 'to remain in the community rather than enter institutional or residential care'. Community care grants may also pay for travelling costs to 'ease a domestic crisis' or to 'attend a relative's funeral'.

These are very broad categories, threatening an open-ended commitment. So, as a first step in managing their budgets, local offices draw up their own lists of priorities. Usually these replicate guidance from the centre, but they also elaborate on it. So, for example, elderly people tend to come top of priority lists, while 'families under stress' tend to come near the bottom - mainly, it seems, because the latter group is perceived to be so large as to threaten a run on the budget if it were given a higher place. Additionally, priority lists may exceptionally specify the items (such as bedding, carpets or cookers) for which grants or loans will be made. Balancing the budget can then be achieved by either lengthening or shortening the list, depending on whether there is money to spare or funds are running out.

Within the constraints of such priority lists, collective office decisions and the budget, individual officers exercise considerable discretion. They can decide whether or not to seek more information from the applicant or to make home visits. They have to make judgements about the ability of applicants to repay loans. More crucially still, they have to determine what is 'genuine need' or what items of furniture or clothing are 'essential' in a process that, as the York study points out, resembles the clinical model of decision-making: moving from analysis to intuition with increasing experience. And the definitions of 'need' and what is 'essential' change with the state of the budget. The result, as Huby and Dix (1992) show, is that not only the chances of an application succeeding vary with the state of the budget but so also does the size of any grant made. In an experimental study social fund officers were asked to make decisions first under budget constraints and then without them. Removing the constraints brought about a 70 per cent reduction in refusal rates and a 28 per cent increase in the size of the awards made.

As predicted, rationing – in a programme marked by the divisibility of the goods being delivered – does indeed take the form of dilution. But, as the evidence of the York study underlines, it also takes the form of denial. Moreover, contrary to our expectations but in line with earlier findings about the role of administrative discretion in the distribution of social welfare payments (Hill 1972) and of 'street level bureaucrats' generally (Lipsky 1980), even relatively low-status officials appear to have considerable scope for adopting their own rationing strategies even within the framework of nationally determined rules.

The next case study, dealing with the allocation of housing by local authorities, is of a rather different kind. First, housing is a less divisible good than money – though there is still some scope for dilution, notably by lowering the quality of the dwellings being allocated. Second, it is an example of second-level priority setting – if within the constraints of national housing policy – since local authorities have autonomy in the way they operate their allocation systems. Third, in what follows, we concentrate on the policies followed by local authorities in making their allocations, rather than the implementation of those policies by officials. In doing so, we draw on a survey carried out by the Institute of Housing (1990).

The rationing of local authority housing starts with deterrence. Few local authorities publicize the system for allocating houses or inform potential applicants about how to apply: a visit to the local authority offices is usually necessary. Next there is rationing by denial: certain groups, like single people without children, are usually ruled out as ineligible unless they are defined as homeless. In most cases, too, residential qualifications are a necessary condition. Finally, there is rationing by delay: if eligible, people are put on the waiting list.

The way in which waiting lists are operated varies greatly. Some authorities operate 'first-come, first-served' systems, i.e. homes go to those who have spent most time on the waiting list. However, other factors may also be considered. These include medical priority, overcrowding, lack of amenities and the number of children. Other authorities operate 'merit' schemes, giving priority to specific groups like the homeless. Most authorities use a points system, weighing the claims of applicants on a number of dimensions. The factors included in such schemes vary, as do the weights given them. So, for example, one authority gives 75 points for someone who has lived in the district for over 15 years, five points for families forced to live apart, for every additional bedroom required and for not having a bathroom or toilet (as well as a variety of other facilities). Additionally, up to 20 points may be awarded by the council's chief technical officer, depending on the condition of the building in which the applicants are living. Another authority gives no points for residency, but gives 40 points if there is one bedroom lacking, 90 points if two are lacking and 150 points if three are lacking, as against ten points for each of the basic amenities (like bathrooms or kitchen facilities) that are lacking. Additionally, it gives points to families with children under 16 living in blocks of flats, with five points if they are on the second floor and 20 points if they are on the fifth floor or above. Finally, the scheme allows up to 40 points to be awarded if current living conditions are considered to be inadequate on inspection.

Most such schemes can be seen as attempts to ration according to need. But, as the above examples show, the concept of need can be interpreted and defined in very different ways. Need may be defined in terms of specific groups, like the homeless, or according to the housing situation of applicants. Different points systems will give a different weighting to families in precisely the same situation (Spicker 1983): a high-priority applicant in one local authority might well be down the list in another. Even when there appears to be a clear national priority, there is much scope for interpretation by local housing departments. For example, the guidance from central government is emphatic that the homeless should have first priority. But there is one proviso: the guidance does not apply to people who make themselves intentionally homeless. And local authorities vary greatly in the way they interpret 'intentionality'. Housing need, in summary, is an elusive concept.

It is precisely because need is such an elusive concept that the allocation of council homes involves at least some discretion in its implementation, a characteristic shared with our first case study. Thus, in both the examples given above, officers have the ability to award 'bonus' points if they consider that current living conditions impose risk or hardship. Indeed, 5 per cent of local authorities explicitly run schemes based on the discretion of officers, while a further 7 per cent operate on the basis of member discretion, i.e. councillors taking the decisions. Interestingly, the retrospective monitoring of how the allocation systems work – and how discretion is used in practice – tends to be rudimentary. To quote the Institute of Housing 1990 study: 'Less than half the authorities presented monitoring information about applicants or offers to councillors. Thus most authorities lacked an important means of being account-able about their handling of allocations and rationing'. In short, the outcome of rationing is largely invisible in the case of council housing, a point to which we shall return when considering health care and the argument that rationing should be carried out by elected rather than nominated authorities.

Finally, housing provides an example of a form of rationing that has so far not been discussed: rationing by 'creaming', as Lipsky (1980) describes it. That is, priority may be given to those who are least likely to give any trouble to the housing department. Thus, some local authorities have ruled out as ineligible those applicants who are in rent arrears or who are deemed to be 'problem families'. Similarly, as noted earlier, there is scope for substitution. Even if those applicants who are perceived to be undesirable, for one reason or another, succeed in qualifying for housing, they may be assigned to the less attractive accommodation owned by the council.

Community care provides another case study of rationing in practice. What follows draws on a survey of local authorities (Association of County Councils/Association of Metropolitan Authorities, 1995). This was based on a questionnaire which asked what care would be allocated to ten different types of applicants, all of whom were elderly people, though in different circumstances. In each case, a profile of the applicants was provided, describing their circumstances. The questionnaire was filled in by an appropriate case manager, i.e. a front-line decision-maker. The result was to demonstrate rationing by exclusion (i.e. by restricting eligibility), by deflection (i.e. shunting the applicant to another service), by substitution (i.e. offering a cheap service in place of a more expensive one) and by dilution (i.e. by limiting the services provided).

There was a large measure of agreement on eligibility, though even this fell short of unanimity. In only half of the 10 cases were most of the respondents agreed that the applicant would be eligible for help. In some cases, the applicants were denied help on the grounds that they would qualify for continuing care in the NHS and hence would not be eligible for local authority care: a classic example of deflection. But the real divergences appeared when it came to deciding what help the applicants should get. So, in the instance of a woman of 90 with a history of heart disease and circulatory problems and living alone, 6 of the respondents would have put her in a nursing home (the most expensive form of care), 23 would have put her in a residential care home (rather less expensive) and 62 would have provided home care. But among those who opted for home care, there were significant differences about how much would be allocated: the range was from 2 hours to over 30 hours per week. Similarly large differences in the amount of home care allocated were apparent in most other cases. Nor is this surprising. To return to our typology of the goods provided by different services, home care (like money) is a classic example of a highly divisible good and offers the greatest scope for rationing by dilution.

Overall, then, these examples drawn from different fields suggest that rationing at the point of service delivery is indeed a pervasive phenomenon in all services that have to manage scarce resources. The mix of strategies followed does differ between services and programmes, but to a lesser extent than might be expected if the decisive factor were the professional status of the decision-makers. Even within programmes where there are national guidelines, as in the case of the Social Fund, the scope for interpretation allows a high discretion to the 'street level bureaucrats'. In services where there are no such guidelines, and where there are local variations in the rules, there is even more scope for differences in the decisions made about who should get what. The common element in all this is that resource allocations reflect judgements about the priorities that should be allocated to competing claimants under budget constraints. In turn, these judgements are shaped by how different kinds of need are perceived. And 'need' turns out to be a Plasticine concept as the evidence reviewed demonstrates: a conclusion whose implications are further explored in the next chapter.

3

PRINCIPLES OF RESOURCE ALLOCATION

So far the emphasis has been on the practice of rationing: the repertory of strategies that may be adopted by those responsible for distributing scarce resources. Some, such as rationing by deterrence or deflection, are mechanisms or expedients which make the fact of rationing less visible. They can be seen as attempts, whether conscious or not, to mask the reality of rationing and to avoid the necessity of making principled decisions as to how resources should be allocated. They are coping strategies pursued by professionals or officials trying to match demand to supply and, by so doing, to make life more tolerable for themselves in what are often difficult circumstances as they strive to keep within their budgets.

But there is, of course, another way of looking at rationing. This is to examine the repertory of principles that is available for designing rationing policies and that helps to shape the strategies adopted. Accordingly, this chapter dips into the pool of normative theory from which those responsible for rationing can draw, whether explicitly or implicitly, in order to identify the criteria that may be used to determine whether a particular rationing process or decision is 'just' or 'fair'. The intention, again, is to look first at the principles embodied in practice in different policy areas (following Elster 1992) before moving on to examining whether or not there are dilemmas specific to health care.

Underlying most rationing practices is some sort of notion of equity defined as allocation according to need. Justice requires that people with equal needs should receive equal treatment, with greater need trumping lesser need. In wartime, rationing, as we have seen, was acceptable precisely because it was seen as being equitable: because it applied to everyone and because the special treatment of some groups (such as more cheese for vegetarians) could be justified in terms of individual needs. Similarly, the allocation systems used by the Social Fund when distributing its cash, by local authorities allocating council housing and by social workers when deciding on who should get what services appear to be shaped by the considerations of equity: the money, the housing or the resources go to those deemed to be in greatest need. Hence the general use of various instruments of assessment designed to ensure that common criteria are applied to everyone, i.e. that everyone's needs are assessed in the same currency. Equity of process, it is assumed, will result in equity of outcome in the distribution of resources.

But, as we have seen in Chapter 2, theory is often betrayed in practice. Decisions are filtered through the perceptions and practices of the professionals and officials. So, for example, the York Study of the Social Fund (Huby and Dix 1992) found that 'there is no evidence that the general needs and circumstances of people receiving awards are clearly distinguishable from those of people who are refused'.

One conclusion that might be drawn from this example, and others, is the familiar one that policy becomes perverted in practice: that the self-interest or biases of service deliverers distort or subvert equity in rationing. If this interpretation were accepted then the difficulties of achieving equity in rationing would be redefined as a problem of policy implementation. The remedy would then lie in devising more sophisticated instruments of assessment, or monitoring, in order to limit discretion in the way rules are translated into decisions in individual cases. But there is another conclusion that may be drawn. This is that, as Lee (1995) has argued, the twin concepts of equity and need provide a fragile and easily fractured foundation for resource allocation because of their inherent ambiguities.

Consider, first, national priority setting decisions. Here neither the concept of equity nor that of need is of much help. In deciding between the competing claims of, say, education and social security, the Cabinet is not generally making equity judgements except, possibly, in the very limited sense of fairness in the allocation of pain between departments. It is making judgements about political expediency, the 'deservingness' of different beneficiaries, the impact on economic performance and so on. To the extent that equity judgements are involved, they are likely to be about the *cumulative* impact of the government's taxing and spending plans on different groups in society. Even this, however, raises the question of how groups should be defined (Rae 1981) when discussing equity between them. Conventionally, analyses of public spending and taxing policies look at the distributional effects by income groups. But there are competing ways of classifying groups. What about equity between the young and the old, between married couples and single people, or between ethnic groups?

The difficulties become compounded if we try to wheel on the concept of need to resolve these difficulties. Disregarding all considerations of political feasibility, it might be argued that equity requires that priority should go to those groups in greatest need. That is (short of a drastic income redistribution policy directing resources to the worst off), spending decisions should reflect the relative needs of those served by the competing services or programmes. If the needs of pensioners are greater than the needs of children, say, then priority should be given to social security over education. But this is to redefine the problem rather than to solve it. It begs the question of whether we have any common currency of comparing the needs of pensioners and children. In the case of pensioners, we might argue that they should be in a position to function as full members of society and to take part in communal life within the constraints of their state of health. To the extent that a proportion of them were unable to meet these conditions, we would be justified in identifying a 'need'. But the concept of need – despite much academic elaboration (see, for example, Braybrooke 1987; Doyal and Gough 1991) – is not a very helpful guide to decision-making. We are still left asking: a need for what? Is it a need for more money, for better health services or for more social support?

Conversely, in the case of children we could argue that they should be able to achieve their full potentials and have an opportunity to develop their talents to the full. To the extent that a proportion of them do not, we would again be justified in identifying a 'need'. Again, however, we have to ask: a need for what? More funding for schools or more resources to change the environment in which the children are growing up? Having identified all these problems, we would still be no nearer to devising a scale for weighing up the relative needs of elderly people as against those of young people to help us in determining priorities between different services and programmes.

But though equity seems to be an unhelpful principle when determining priorities at the national level, it plays an important part in determining the distribution of funds from central government to the intermediate levels. Central government grants to local authorities are based on the principle that all such authorities should have an equal ability to satisfy the needs of their populations at any given level of resource availability. The formula used has gone through a variety of permutations over the decades and is now incarnated in the Standard Spending Assessment, which determines the distribution of central government funds to local authorities. The aim is to achieve equity by taking account of both the revenue raising capacity of the authorities and the needs of their populations. The future costs of providing specific services are deduced from past levels of expenditure – a somewhat unsatisfactory proxy for need (Audit Commission 1993) – and regression analysis is used to provide appropriate weightings for the factors, such as the demographic composition of the population, that are included in the formula. As we shall see, a similar formula is used to allocate funds in the NHS.

All this might suggest that the concept of need is sturdier, and more useful for the allocation of resources, than our previous discussion suggested. But this might be a premature conclusion. The operational definition and measurement of need in all such formulae tend to be highly contentious. Moreover, an alternative interpretation is possible and is highly significant for the practice of rationing in general. This is that equity is embraced as the guiding principle for distributing resources geographically for precisely the same reasons that it is rejected when it comes to prioritizing between different services and programmes at the national level. It is because it is so difficult to use equity-based-on-need to determine priorities at the national level that responsibility for determining the allocation of funds between competing services and programmes is pushed down to the level below. For the assumption in doing so is that nearness to the population being served will allow those responsible for allocating resources to the service delivery level to make a more sensitive choice between different spending options: to interpret need in the light of the local context. And, as we have seen, local authorities do indeed make very different choices as to the priorities to be accorded to different groups. Different answers may also be given to the question of what a specific need is for: there is scope for substitutability between services and programmes. Different local authority may respond to the same 'need' either by offering housing or by providing social support.

There is a further assumption implicit in this process of downward delegation. This is that the process of decision-making is as important as the principles guiding it: that decisions about resource allocation gain their legitimacy not from abstract principles of justice but from the fact that they are taken by elected members accountable to their populations. The justification for pushing down decision-making is, in short, the assumption that priorities should reflect the preferences of the populations being served – preferences which may or may not be in accord with the equity principle. There are many problems about this line of argument, to which we shall return when considering health care, where it is often argued (Harrison and Hunter 1994) that rationing decisions lack legitimacy because they are not taken by elected members. Here it is sufficient to note that democratic processes are not necessarily an effective way of aggregating preferences (Weale 1990). Nor do they guarantee accountability (Day and Klein 1987): as the example of housing allocations, cited in Chapter 2, showed, the process may be extremely opaque even in local authorities which are supposedly accountable to their electorate. The important point, at this stage of our analysis, is that looking at the 'justice' of allocative decisions provides only one perspective on rationing and that there are alternative, process-related criteria of justification.

To stress the difficulties of giving meaning to the concept of 'need' is to explain also, in part at least, the further delegation of decision-making to the third level, i.e. to the professionals and officials responsible for the allocation of services to individuals at the point of service delivery – rationing in the strict sense. Once we accept the problematic nature of the concepts of equity and need – and the difficulties involved in trying to operationalize them – then the use of discretion at the point of service delivery becomes not a perversion of policy in the process of implementation but a rational response to the difficulty of devising decision-making rules that are sufficiently specific and robust to cope with all contingencies. Just as the case for pushing responsibility from the national level to the local level rests on the argument that need can only be interpreted in context – taking account of specific circumstances – so the argument for pushing responsibility down from the local level to the service deliverers rests on the argument that only they can interpret the complexity of individual circumstances. Discretion, in short, is a function of ambiguity. And considerations of equity revolve primarily around the way in which that discretion is exercised: it becomes a process criterion, where the currency of evaluation is freedom from bias and the absence of arbitrariness in the allocatory judgements made.

ALTERNATIVE RATIONING CRITERIA

Given that equity is an uncertain guide to rationing, a Delphic oracle often speaking in riddles open to conflicting interpretations, it is not surprising that a variety of other principles are often invoked – tacitly or explicitly – in making allocatory decisions. In what follows we review these briefly and selectively, distinguishingly between two categories of arguments: those whose starting point is the characteristic of the individuals concerned and those whose focus is on the collective good (for general reviews, see Elster 1992; Chadwick 1993). In the first category come notions of desert or merit. Priority in resource allocation, in this view, should go to those who have 'earned' special consideration. This might be because, like elderly people, they have paid taxes and been good citizens for a lifetime. Or it might be because they are outstanding in their talents: because they are brilliant mathematicians or musicians. Clearly considerations like these colour at least some rationing decisions. In the case of the Social Fund, for example, the evidence suggests that elderly people are treated more generously than other types of applicants. Conversely, however, it might be argued that children deserve priority because, unlike old people, they have not had a chance to fulfil their potentials. And, again, there is evidence that this consideration shapes resource allocation within some programmes, such as social services, where priority is often given to spending on children rather than the elderly.

Need also creeps back into considerations about how to allocate resources according to the characteristics of the individuals concerned, but in a rather different way from that previously discussed. Priority in resource allocation should go, it may be said, to those who are at greatest risk: need, in other words, is assessed in terms of the consequences if resources are not allocated. Here the criterion is the degree of risk of deterioration in the situation of those concerned in the absence of action (be it a Social Fund grant, social work intervention or medical help). The implications of taking this view may be very different from those that flow from the standard argument for allocating resources according to need. The latter requires priority in resource allocation to go to those whose welfare deficit (on some scale or other) is greatest: 'to individuals at the lowest pre-allocative welfare level', to quote Elster (1992). But degree of risk is not necessarily the same as degree of need. Two individuals may have precisely the same needs – measured in terms of their welfare level – but one may be at greater risk of deterioration than the other. If so, then, following this line of reasoning, priority in resource allocation should go to whoever is most at risk of suffering damage in the absence of action. Risk assessment is similar to need assessment, however, in one important respect. It tends to push decision-making about rationing to the periphery, i.e. it is only service deliverers who have the information required to make a judgement about relative degrees of risk.

There is a further twist to this line of reasoning. Assume that two people not only are at the same welfare level but also have the same degree of risk. Who should have priority? Here a further principle is usually invoked: the capacity to benefit. Resources should go, it is argued, to whoever is likely to benefit most as a result of intervention. To invoke this principle is, however, to move from considerations about the characteristics of the individuals concerned to considerations about the use of societal resources. The assumption is that scarce resources should be allocated in ways that will maximize the benefits not to individuals but to society as a whole. We are in the territory of utilitarian analysis (in its many forms), where the focus is on comparing the increments of benefits yielded by resource allocation decisions. The emphasis is on the consequences of allocating (or denying) resources rather than the degree of need or risk *ex ante*. It is the value added by intervention the gain in terms of harm prevented or an improved ability to function – that becomes the principle guiding rationing. Enter, in short, the classic economist's notion of opportunity costs translated into the ethical imperative of maximizing the welfare of society as a whole. As Williams (1992) has argued, 'anyone who says that no account should be paid to costs is really saying that no account should be paid to the sacrifices imposed on others'. It is unethical, in short, to ignore costs.

Even to demonstrate that a specific individual has a high degree of risk or need is therefore not sufficient, in this view, to justify giving him or her priority in resource allocation. Nor, indeed, is it enough to demonstrate that such an individual would benefit as a result of having resources allocated to him or her. What has to be demonstrated is that those resources could not be put to better use elsewhere. From this perspective, the crucial question is not so much whether resources allocated to a particular individual would or would not improve his or her condition, but whether those same resources would produce an even bigger increment in welfare if applied elsewhere or used for someone else. Collective needs or gains come before individual needs or gains.

This perspective shifts the focus of resource allocation decisions from the characteristics of individuals to the characteristics of the groups (defined by their being candidates for a particular service or programme) to which those individuals belong. It involves asking questions about the comparative benefits yielded by different categories of intervention for those groups. It directs attention as much towards those who may not be in the queue for services as to questions of prioritizing between those already in the queue. In doing so, it challenges the primacy of service deliverers in making rationing decisions. For if maximizing collective welfare trumps maximizing individual benefits, then it is information about the impact of specific resource allocation policies rather than information about the characteristics of individual would-be beneficiaries that becomes crucial. In other words, adopting a utilitarian approach (using this term in a loose, non-technical sense) affects, potentially at least, not only the criteria used in taking decisions about priorities but also the distribution of decision-making power. It promises to shift control back to the centre by bringing a new set of actors on to the stage as a counterweight to the professionals and officials involved in the service delivery process: economists and others expert in the analysis of the 'yield', in terms of welfare benefits, of different resource allocation policies.

To make this point is, however, to beg a crucial question. This is whether it is possible to devise a currency to measure – and compare on a common numerator – the benefits yielded. This is a matter of much dispute among economists and others. Rather than allowing ourselves to be sucked into the bog of disciplinary controversy, we shall illustrate the kind of problems encountered by examining the attempt to quantify the benefits of different patterns of resource allocation in the particular case of health care as exemplified by the development of Quality Adjusted Life Years (QALYs). Conceptually QALYs are elegant in their simplicity. Take a particular form of therapy, say a hip replacement or a kidney transplant, then look at the number of years that a patient can expect to survive, weighted by the quality of life that can be expected. The 'yield' of different forms of intervention can then be calculated in terms of the cost per QALY gained.

We shall explore the robustness and usefulness (or otherwise) of QALYs in the context of NHS priority setting in Chapter 10. Here we simply note what is perhaps the most fundamental objection raised to using such tools for determining priorities. This is that interventions designed to save lives cannot be measured on the same scale as interventions designed to improve the quality of life. Thus, it has been argued that 'Most people think, and for good as well as prudential reasons, that life saving has priority over life enhancement and that we should first allocate resources to those areas where they are immediately needed to save life; only when this has been done should the remainder be allocated to alleviating non-fatal conditions' (Harris 1988).

This objection has particular force in the case of health care. But it begs a crucial question, with relevance for other fields of decision-making about scarce resources such as child protection. Is saving life an open-ended cheque? Here practice suggests the importance of distinguishing between visible and statistical lives (Weale 1979): that is, between interventions designed to save a particular, identifiable life and interventions designed to lessen the statistical risk of some anonymous person dying in future in the absence of action. The evidence suggests that visible lives tend to be given a higher degree of priority in resource allocation over statistical lives; that present danger is given greater weight – in terms of a readiness to spend money in order to avert it – than future risk. There appears to be a greater readiness to mount spectacular (and expensive) operations to rescue a stranded mountaineer than to invest, for example, in preventive measures such as paying GPs to give advice about stopping smoking – even though the QALY yield of the latter appears to be an exceptionally good bargain (Maynard 1994).

Within a utilitarian framework of analysis this seems to be a perverse and irrational way of allocating scarce resources. But is it? The perversity and irrationality become not only comprehensible but, in theory at least, justifiable if we assume – following the arguments of Philippe d'Iribarne (1969) – that one of the outputs of any system of social protection is a collective sense of security. Any evaluation of the costs of different forms of social intervention should therefore take into account 'the satisfaction that society takes in seeing these actions accomplished'. If we could measure the 'utilities' of those who draw satisfaction from seeing lives saved through dramatic or heroic interventions, we might draw up a very different balance sheet from one based only on the experience of the individuals directly involved.

But, in conclusion, it is important to stress once again that utilitarianism is only one of a set of competing theories invoked in decision-making about priority setting and rationing. Many, like utilitarianism itself, apply across services and programmes. So, for example, the Rawlsian 'difference principle' (Rawls 1972) can be invoked to argue that priority in resource allocation should be given to the most disadvantaged (Harrison 1995). Differences (or inequalities) are only justified, in this view, if they benefit the most disadvantaged; maximizing the welfare of the worst off thus has priority over maximizing the welfare of the population as a whole. Pareto optimality, *contra* the utilitarians, is not enough. Other theories, while not necessarily unique to health care, are invoked with special resonance in the case of medicine: in particular those which stress the responsibility of the individual doctor to the individual patient as part of the professional ethic. The patient's trust in the doctor imposes a corresponding obligation on the practitioner to do his or her best for that patient. In the words of the General Medical Council's (1995) guidance to good medical practice, 'You should always seek to give priority to the investigation and treatment of patients solely on the basis of need.' However, the General Medical Council also acknowledges that, given resource constraints, doctors must recognize 'the effects their decisions may have on the resources and choices available to others' (British Medical Association, 1995).

The ethical imperative to do the utmost for the individual patient, regardless of cost-benefit calculations, is encapsulated in what has been called the 'rule of rescue'. As Jonsen (1986) argues, 'Our moral response to the imminence of death demands that we rescue the doomed. We throw a rope to the drowning, rush into burning buildings to snatch the entrapped, dispatch teams to search for the snowbound. This rescue morality spills into medical care, where our ropes are artificial hearts, our rush is the mobile critical care unit, our teams are the transplant service.' In short, the commands of morality may – in life-and-death situations at least – contradict the calculations of cost–benefit analysis.

This chapter has identified some of the conflicting ways of arguing about priority setting and rationing. In the chapters that follow we explore further how they are used – whether explicitly or implicitly – in the NHS.

PART II

THE NHS EXPERIENCE

4

THE NHS: A HISTORY
OF INSTITUTIONALIZED
SCARCITY

The National Health Service was the child of scarcity, conceived at a time when Britain was still recovering from the ravages of war. It has remained a monument to institutionalized scarcity ever since. No sooner had the NHS been launched in 1948 than it was overtaken by a series of expenditure crises (Webster 1988). The estimates of its cost, prepared in advance of its creation, proved as over-optimistic as they were crude. Year by year, Aneurin Bevan, the Minister of Health and the NHS's architect, had to ask his colleagues in the Labour government's Cabinet for extra money to cover the budget overshoot. In its first year, the original estimate of £150 million was exceeded by £50 million; in its second year, the original estimate of £260 million was exceeded by £60 million. The issue became a matter of a continuing and increasingly acrimonious Cabinet debate as spending appeared to be out of control and as Bevan resisted proposals for limiting demand and raising extra revenue by introducing charges.

Bevan's case, foreshadowing future debates about the NHS's finances, was simple. 'The plain fact is that the cost of the hospital service not only will, but ought to, increase', he told his Cabinet colleagues in a memorandum (Minister of Health 1950). 'Most of the hospitals fall far short of any proper standard. . . . Also it is in this field, particularly, that constant new developments will always be needed to keep pace with research progress (as recently, in penicillin, streptomycin, cortisone etc.) and to expand essential specialist services'. It was certainly possible to restrain expenditure, he concluded, but only if the Cabinet was prepared to accept the consequences, which would be that 'people needing treatment must be turned away, beds closed and the service curtailed'.

The Cabinet was not convinced by these arguments. The Treasury triumphed. The Cabinet imposed a ceiling of £400 million on the NHS budget and accepted that charges would have to be introduced – the latter decision leading to Bevan's resignation from the government. So was enshrined the principle that has continued to govern the NHS's funding ever since. The budget of the NHS was not to be determined by demand or need but by Cabinet decisions about the allocation of resources between competing claims from other government departments within the limits set by the imperatives of economic management. Once these decisions had been made, the NHS would have to operate within the fixed budget that had been set for it. It was a principle which also implied (although this was never explicitly stated) that, if necessary, 'people needing treatment' might indeed have to be turned away.

The Minister of Health had a statutory obligation to provide an 'adequate service'. But how was adequacy to be defined and translated into budgetary decisions? Then, as now, the question proved impossible to answer. The Committee of Enquiry into the Cost of the NHS (Guillebaud 1956) – appointed in 1953 by the Conservative government that succeeded the Labour administration – was emphatic on this point. It argued that:

> If the test of 'adequacy' were that the Service should be able to meet every demand which is justifiable on medical grounds, then the Service is clearly inadequate now, and very considerable additional expenditure (both capital and current) would be required to make it so. . . . To make the Service fully 'adequate' . . . a greatly increased share of the nation's human and material resources would have to be diverted to it from other resources.

In any case, the Committee pointed out, the notion of 'adequacy' was itself elusive:

> But even if it were possible, which we very much doubt, to attach a specific meaning to the term 'an adequate service' at a given moment of time, it does not follow that it would remain so for long with merely normal replacement. There is no stability in the concept itself: what might have been held to be adequate twenty years ago would no longer be so regarded today, while today's standards will in turn become out of date

in the future. The advance of medical knowledge continually places new demands on the Service, and the standards expected by the public also continue to rise.

Given this, the Committee concluded that: 'in the absence of an objective and attainable standard of adequacy, the aim must be, as in the field of education, to provide the best service possible within the limits of the available resources'.

The arguments of the Guillebaud Committee have been quoted extensively because they encapsulate the dilemma of the NHS. Little has changed since it reported. Given that it is a predominantly tax-financed service, political and economic considerations inevitably constrain the ability of the NHS to respond to demand. Not surprisingly, its conclusions were, in essence, echoed more than 20 years later by the Royal Commission on the NHS (Merrison 1979). No health service, it argued, could satisfy all the demands made upon it. From this it followed that 'it is misleading to pretend that the NHS can meet all expectations. Hard choices have to be made. It is a prime duty of those concerned in the provision of health care to make it clear to the rest of us what we can reasonably expect'.

But 'reasonable expectations' have never been defined. Attempts to use the courts to compel the NHS to provide specific services have invariably failed. When in 1977 patients in the queue for orthopaedic surgery sought a judicial declaration that the Secretary of State had failed in his statutory duty of providing a comprehensive health service, the trial judge ruled against them. The decision was upheld on appeal, on the ground that the Secretary of State had done his best 'with the financial resources available to him' and that it was not for the courts to question his policies (Miller 1992). Indeed, the courts have consistently rejected all attempts to introduce any notion of entitlements in the NHS (Longley 1993).

Nor has this situation changed greatly as the result of the publication of *The Patient's Charter* (Secretary of State for Health 1991). This set out, for the first time, the 'rights' of patients. But these rights were expressed in somewhat limited terms: waiting times for outpatient appointments and in outpatient clinics, respect for privacy and dignity and ease of access to services for those with disabilities. They were about access to NHS facilities, not about access to specific forms of treatment. Essentially, then, one of the defining characteristics of the NHS – in contrast to many other health care systems – remains its repudiation of any notion of entitlements. Patients may have a right of access to health care, but, once access has been achieved, it is for providers to decide what treatment (if any) to offer within the constraints of the available resources.

RESOURCES AND RATIONING: THE EARLY DECADES

The 1950s were years of austerity for the NHS. Expenditure on the NHS, far from being increased in order to deal with the inadequacies recognized by Guillebaud and everyone else, fell both as a proportion of the gross domestic product (GDP) and in absolute terms. Only towards the end of the decade did spending levels start inching upward. Not until the mid-1960s did expenditure, as a percentage of GDP, reach the level achieved in 1950: 4.2 per cent. By then spending on the NHS, at constant prices, was some 50 per cent higher than it had been at the time of the 1950 Cabinet wrangles (Merrison 1979: Tables E6–E8). Thereafter, albeit with many hiccups, expenditure was set on an upward path, topping 7 per cent of GDP by the mid-1990s.

The salience of rationing as an issue for political and public debate did not, however, reflect the expenditure trajectory of the NHS. Paradoxically, there was little – if any – public discussion of rationing in the early years when the NHS budget was most hard-pressed. The paradox is more apparent than real, but suggests an important conclusion. This is that political and public perceptions about rationing are not necessarily a function of the balance between supply and demand but rather reflect the balance between supply and expectations. If expectations are low, as they were in the early decades of the NHS, then any 'inadequacies' are likely to be perceived and accepted as part of the natural order of things.

· There was, of course, awareness that NHS resources were stretched and that new demands were threatening to overwhelm it. When a conference was held to celebrate the twentieth anniversary of the NHS's creation, there was much discussion of the stresses caused both by new technology, creating new opportunities to deal with hitherto untreatable conditions, and by the burden of chronic disease, accentuated by the ageing of the population (Department of Health and Social Security 1968). But the main theme of the various conference contributions was the need to improve efficiency in order to make the available resources go further. There was no discussion of rationing as such. Moreover, this was a debate among insiders. The searchlight of media attention to the NHS had not been switched on.

One voice, however, did raise the dread word. With his usual insistence on saying what others thought best left unsaid, Enoch Powell (1966) brought the issue out into the open in his reflections on his experience as Minister of Health in the early 1960s. Rationing was inevitable, he argued, given that the supply of resources was limited and that demand was not constrained by price: hence the phenomenon of waiting lists, the most pervasive and palpable (in Powell's words) form of rationing. Further, he wrote, in words that still carry resonance 30 years later:

> The task is not made easier by the political convention that the existence of any rationing at all must be strenuously denied. The public are encouraged to believe that rationing in medical care was banished by the National Health Service, and that the very idea of rationing being applied to medical care is immoral and repugnant. Consequently when they, and the medical profession too, come face to face in practice with the various forms of rationing to which the National Health Service must resort, the usual result is bewilderment, frustration and irritation.

From this he drew the conclusion that: 'The worst kind of rationing is that which is unacknowledged; for it is the essence of a good rationing system to be intelligible and consciously accepted. This is not possible where its very existence has to be repudiated'.

But its existence did continue to be repudiated and, as we shall see, continues to be repudiated to this day. In the mid-1970s a book entitled *Rationing Health Care* (Cooper 1975) was published. But it had little resonance. And this was despite the fact that waiting lists were far from being the only form of rationing. In addition to such rationing by delay, the NHS also practised rationing by denial. The point is well illustrated by the example of treatment for kidney failure (end stage renal disease). The story is well told by Thomas Halper (1989) and in what follows we draw on his account. Haemodialysis first began to be used, on an experimental basis, in the early 1960s. By the mid-1960s, a dozen small centres in the UK were using this technique. Here was, as Halper puts it, a technology that was fairly reliable, that was lifesaving and that was expensive. If its adoption were left unchecked, the financial implications for the NHS were very considerable. So how was its use to be controlled? In 1965, the Ministry of Health asked the President of the Royal

College of Physicians to convene a conference of consultants to advise on the matter, the first of a series of advisory committees. The outcome was a policy of restricting renal dialysis to a limited number of regional centres funded directly from the centre. It was, in all but name, a strategy of rationing scarce resources. But it was justified not in terms of the resource implications of letting the new technology take off unchecked but by medical considerations about the desirability of concentrating expertise.

Subsequently, the technology of treating kidney failure developed. Home dialysis increasingly replaced the more expensive hospital dialysis; kidney transplants increasingly replaced dialysis. The number of renal units – and of specialists – crept up. The Department of Health, as it had become, raised its targets for the number of people who should be treated. Even so, resource constraints – compounded by a shortage of kidneys for transplants – continued to limit the number of people treated. By the mid–1980s (Feest *et al.* 1990) the number of patients under age 60 per million inhabitants treated in Britain was roughly similar to that in most other West European countries. But the number of over–60s was much fewer. As one specialist in the field concluded, 'older patients, and those with multisystem diseases, notably diabetes, have been squeezed out of our treatment programmes' (Wing 1990). The result was that, even by the mid-1990s, Britain still only ranked twenty-first in the European league table of new patients receiving treatment every year: behind every European country with the exception of Bulgaria (Kingman 1996)

In effect, therefore, people whose lives could have been saved – and would have been saved if they lived in other countries – died. It was rationing of a very brutal kind. But it was not perceived as such. The British Kidney Patient Association campaigned vigorously – and, to an extent, successfully – for more resources. However, this campaign did not lead to any wider public debate about 'rationing' in the NHS. Political decisions about the allocation of resources had been successfully transmuted into clinical decisions about who should be treated: a point to which we return when discussing the role of the medical profession in rationing.

The precedent set by renal dialysis was followed when other new and expensive life-saving technologies became available in the 1980s. When heart and liver transplantation became feasible, the Department of Health's Chief Medical Officer (1987) again took the initiative in engineering a professional consensus about the rate of development. The number of centres for carrying out these procedures was limited. In contrast to the situation in the United States – and some other countries – the introduction of the new technologies was strictly controlled, so inevitably limiting access and restricting the availability of the procedure. It was rationing but was not perceived as such because it appeared to be dictated not by resource constraints but by technical, professional considerations about the state of the art and the desirability of concentrating expertise in a few centres. The link between government decisions about priorities – the allocation of resources both to the NHS and to specific areas within it – and the impact of rationing in terms of decisions about individual patients had still to be made in public debate.

SETTING PRIORITIES

If the language of rationing did not feature much in debates about the NHS until the 1990s, the vocabulary of priorities came into use much earlier. In the second half of the 1970s the Department of Health and Social Security published two documents setting out its priorities (Secretary of State for Social Services 1976, 1977). The first – issued under the regime of Barbara Castle – was a consultation document. The second, *The Way Forward* – issued by her successor as Secretary of State, David Ennals – set out the policy conclusions. Both reflected the realization that the welfare state could no longer live off the dividends of the growth state (Klein 1975). The global economic crisis of the mid-1970s had put an end to the era of optimism about sustained growth and the Labour government was seeking to halt the rise in public expenditure. The Department of Health faced the prospect of a reduced growth rate for its budget. In a service 'where demand will always outstrip our capacity to meet it', to quote Mrs Castle's foreword to the first document, 'choice is never easy, but choose we must'.

For our purposes, two aspects of these documents are of special interest. The first is that, unsurprisingly given that this was a resource allocation exercise, priorities were expressed in terms of inputs. Different services, it was proposed, should expand at different rates. The aim was to achieve a new balance in the distribution of NHS resources. Specifically, services for the elderly and for the mentally ill and handicapped were to have a larger annual increment of growth than acute services. Success would be measured by the increase in the number of available beds and the supporting manpower. There was no attempt to translate the distribution of resources into targets for improving the availability or accessibility of specific services. It was not until the 1980s, when the emphasis of government policy switched to outcomes, that the Department of Health began to set targets in terms of the number of operations that should be carried out or of waiting times.

The second is that the priorities set out in the two documents reflect a dimension of rationing which has so far not been discussed in this chapter. The examples of rationing so far cited – such as waiting lists and limited access to life saving technology – are specific to the acute services. They are rationing by delay or by denial. But the priority documents were designed to address a very different form of rationing: by dilution. Throughout the 1960s and the early 1970s, a series of inquiries into scandals at long-stay hospitals (Martin 1984) had revealed appallingly poor conditions in many institutions. The result was to give visibility to rationing by dilution, although the dread word was never used. And the priority documents can be seen, in part at least, as a response to this revelation – although, clearly, other considerations were also involved, notably the ageing of the population and the increasing emphasis on developing community services to replace institutional care. They were an acknowledgment – if only implicit – that decades of low priority for spending on services for the elderly, the mentally ill and handicapped had produced an unacceptable degree of rationing.

There is, clearly, an important conceptual distinction between forms of rationing that delay or deny services to specific individuals and one which results in a low quality of provision delivered in a poor environment for everyone using a particular service. The common element, however, is that in both cases patients receive less than either they or NHS professionals may think is desirable – or, in the case of long-stay institutions, acceptable to society. The priorities of the two 1970s documents are a reminder, therefore, that to discuss rationing exclusively in terms of access to specific forms of medical intervention is to miss half the story. The other half of the story is the quality of care offered once access has been achieved. The implications of this distinction are profound. For while the demand for medical intervention, in the strict sense, may be limited – after all, the time may come when everyone has had hips replaced – it is not self-evident that the demand for care in the wider sense and an improved environment for its delivery necessarily has a ceiling. The point is crucial and we shall have frequent occasion to return to it in our subsequent discussion.

THE GEOGRAPHY OF RESOURCE ALLOCATION

The 1970s also saw a further development which illuminates yet another dimension of rationing so far not discussed: the geographical dimension. A number of studies in the early 1970s (for example, Logan *et al.* 1972) demonstrated the existence of wide variations in the availability of services in the regions of the NHS. These mirrored, in turn, wide variations in the budgets allocated to regional health authorities. These budgets did not appear to reflect differences in the health or social conditions of the populations concerned but the system of allocation in the early decades of the NHS, when the formula seemed to be 'What you got last year, plus an allowance for growth, plus an allowance for scandals' (Maynard and Ludbrook 1980). This clearly represented a challenge to the principle of distributional equity, for how could there be equal access for equal need if different parts of the NHS were unequally endowed? A necessary, if not sufficient, condition for ensuring fairness in the allocation of resources to individuals appeared to be missing.

There followed a series of attempts to find a formula which would allocate resources equitably, i.e. according to need. The most significant of these was the RAWP formula produced by the Resource Allocation Working Party (1976), from which it took its acronym. Need, in this formula, was measured (to oversimplify) by the demographic composition of the population and standardized mortality ratios. The latter, it was argued, represented the best available proxy for morbidity. The result was to produce a budget target for each of the regions; progress towards these targets was to be achieved by a process of differential growth in their annual spending allocations. To a large extent the aim of bringing about greater equity in the distribution of resources – as defined by the RAWP formula – was achieved. However, it is important to note two limitations of the RAWP formula. First, it only purported to measure *relative* need. It was designed to achieve distributional fairness only and had nothing to say about the adequacy of the allocations that resulted. Second, it only covered expenditure on hospital and community services, not primary care.

The resource allocation formula was subsequently fine-tuned. In particular, following the 1991 reforms, it was adapted for use in making weighted capitation allocations to individual health authorities at the sub-regional level. For our purposes, the most significant feature of all these attempts is that the debate about the design of a formula has become an increasingly arcane dialogue among statisticians and other methodological experts (for an authoritative review, see Mays 1995). As in the case of the original RAWP formula, there was much argument about the relationship between mortality and need. If a region had a standardized mortality ratio (SMR) of 110 did this mean that it should receive 10 per cent more resources than an area with an SMR of 100? Or should it be 5 per cent? Similarly, there was much discussion as to whether the formula should include a weighting for social deprivation. Most recently, the University of York (Carr-Hill *et al.* 1994) produced a new formula based on the utilization of services, while trying to meet the criticism that utilization reflects supply rather than need with some heroic, highly sophisticated statistical manipulations. The formula, which would have favoured health authorities in the north of England at the expense of those in the south, was subsequently modified by ministers in order to soften the impact of redistribution (Peacock and Smith 1995).

All in all, therefore, the attempts to devise a formula for distributing resources in the NHS – to achieve equity in geographical rationing, as it were – share many of the characteristics of the Standard Spending Assessment (SSA) used for allocating resources to local authorities (see above), and for much the same reason. This is that need is an elusive concept, all the more so because past patterns of utilization may be a poor guide for the future. As Mays (1995) has pointed out: '"Need" for health care resources in the context of making fair allocations to different areas depends on judgment about which features of human suffering we believe it is worth responding to through the health care system'. No amount of statistical ingenuity can substitute for such judgements. And the main result of deploying ever more methodological sophistication is – as in the case of the SSA – twofold. First, it makes the resulting formula ever more difficult to comprehend and ever more difficult to justify to a wider, non-expert audience. Second, and following on from this, ministers are likely to judge a formula not by its methodological rigour but by its consequences. The greater the statistical sophistication and its consequent public impermeability, the greater will be the opportunities (and temptation) for political manipulation.

In addition to the problems of devising a resource distribution formula that is both technically sound and politically acceptable, there is a fundamental ambiguity about what this approach is supposed to achieve. Is it meant merely to equalize the capacity of health authorities to respond to the needs – however defined – of the population in their area, while leaving those authorities freedom how to interpret those needs and how to translate them into specific service provision? Or is it meant to equalize access to specific services and to bring about the equal provision of treatment for those populations by ensuring that the same package of health care is available everywhere? These questions are, as we shall see, crucial for the practice of rationing. But they have never been answered definitively and successive governments have been consistent only in their determination to evade them.

This evasion reflects a tension evident throughout the history of the NHS: the tension between centralization and devolution, between the decentralization of credit and the diffusion of blame (Klein 1995). Governments, irrespective of political party, have sought to claim credit for themselves for positive achievements (such as an increase in the number of operations carried out or in the numbers of patients treated), while also making it clear that they believed in local decision-making and could therefore not be blamed for any shortcomings that resulted from such decisions. The result has been a manic-depressive cycle in which periods of centralization alternate with periods of devolution.

The dilemma was neatly summed up by Barbara Castle in her 1976 document:

> Ever since I became Secretary of State, health authorities and local authorities have been pressing for less central intervention in day to day management and I have readily accepted that more devolution of detailed decision-making must take place. At the same time, as Minister responsible for the National Health Service and for guiding the personal social services, I have a duty to set national policy guidelines within which local needs are assessed.

The same theme was taken up by Patrick Jenkin, the Secretary of State for Social Services, in the Conservative administration that succeeded the Labour government in 1979. His document on priorities (Secretary of State for Social Services 1981) did not signal a change as far as the substance of policy was concerned: again the emphasis was on giving priority to services for the elderly, the mentally ill and handicapped. But there was a subtle change of emphasis in the way he presented them to the members of district health authorities:

> This handbook sets out the main policies and priorities which
> Ministers will look to you to follow in running the services for
> which you are responsible. We want to give you as much
> freedom as possible to decide how to pursue these policies and
> priorities in your own locality. Local initiatives, local decisions,
> and local responsibility are what we want to encourage. . . .
> You have therefore a wider opportunity than your prede-
> cessors to plan and develop services in the light of *local* needs
> and circumstances.

The era of devolution was not to last long. The emphasis switched
from inputs to outputs, from the allocation of resources to specific
services to the performance of those services in terms of what was
being offered to patients. By the mid-1980s (Day and Klein 1985)
the Department of Health and Social Security was setting performance targets to the regions: for example, the number of open heart
operations to be carried out and the number of patients to be
offered renal dialysis. It was a trend that was to continue, with
central government setting targets for the number of hip replacements and coronary artery by-pass grafts, as well as waiting times
(Secretary of State for Health 1992a). The main change came in the
1990s, when the emphasis switched from outputs to outcomes
subsequent to the publication of *The Health of the Nation* (Secretary
of State for Health 1992b). Now priorities and targets were specified
in terms not only of desired outputs but also of desired effects on the
population's health (Secretary of State for Health 1993). So, for
example, the 25 targets included to reduce deaths as a result of
coronary heart disease among the under–65s by at least 40 per cent
and the suicide rate by 15 per cent, and to cut the incidence of
obesity and smoking in the population. Prevention, in short, had
become a top priority.

Although priority talk changed, the underlying tension was not
resolved. Precisely because need is such an elusive concept – to
return to one of our major themes – national priorities were still left
to health authorities to interpret and to implement in the light of
local circumstances. The next chapter further explores this theme
by examining, first, how central government formulated its priorities in the years following the 1991 reforms of the NHS and,
second, how health authorities set about the task of implementing
them.

5

PRIORITY SETTING IN
THE NEW ERA

The 1991 reforms of the NHS, first set out in *Working for Patients* (Secretary of State for Health 1989), transformed the context of decision-making about the allocation of resources. In future, district health authorities were no longer to be responsible for running services. They were to become purchasers, free to buy the services needed by their populations and to shop around among competing providers. In turn, providers were to become independent trusts directly accountable to the Secretary of State. The budgets of purchasers would be determined by a weighted capitation formula. The budgets of providers would depend on their ability to attract business. The relationship between district health authorities and providers would therefore no longer be hierarchic, as in the past, but would be based on contracts specifying what was to be bought and at what price. The dynamics of market competition would thus be injected into what remained a publicly funded system. So was born the NHS's mimic market.

The 1991 reforms were more complex, of course, than this brief summary suggests. In particular, the purchasing role was split between health authorities and general practitioner fundholders. Such fundholding GPs were allocated budgets from which to buy the services needed by their patients. By April 1995, some two-fifths of the population were signed up with GP fundholders. But since GP budgets covered only a restricted range of services – although this was to expand subsequently – their total expenditure accounted for only 8 per cent of total spending on hospital and community services (Audit Commission 1995b). The scope of purchasing by GP fundholders therefore remains limited, and in what follows we concentrate on the role of health authorities as allocators of resources.

The most significant aspect of this role, from the perspective of this study, is that the 1991 reforms implied a very different approach to resource allocation from previous practice. In the past, the starting point for budgetary decisions had been the needs of the providers for which the health authorities were responsible. Now the starting point was to be the needs of the population for whom the health authorities were responsible. Purchasing was to be population-driven, not provider-driven. Health authorities would assess the needs of their populations and then choose among the competing claims for resources. Decisions about resource allocation would therefore have to become more explicit as health authorities chose what package of health care to buy and what not to buy. And the decisions would be all the more transparent, since health authorities were required to publish their annual purchasing plans.

That, at any rate, was the assumption. In the event, as we shall see, the mists were slow to clear. Decisions about priorities in spending – and the consequences for rationing at the point of service delivery – have so far been neither as explicit nor as transparent as expected. In this chapter, we set out the evidence for this assertion, while in the following we analyse in greater depth the reasons for this apparent failure to follow the logic of the 1991 reforms. Before doing so, however, we examine the environment and context in which health authorities were making their resource allocation decisions and the guidance provided by the Department of Health.

THE NHS'S AGE OF ANXIETY

The NHS, in its new post–1991 incarnation, was an organization striving for stability but never quite achieving it. Setting up the new system required a major investment of effort, dislocating existing ways of working and creating much turbulence for all those engaged in running it. New information systems had to be invented; the skills of negotiating and writing contracts had to be learnt; the consequences of switching business from one provider to another had to be explored. And no sooner had the NHS overcome the problems involved in setting up the new system than the system itself changed yet again. District health authorities were amalgamated and rechristened health commissions. In turn the health commissions were amalgamated with the family health authorities responsible

for primary health care. The regional health authorities disappeared, to become regional offices of the Department of Health.
There were other kinds of change as well. Market competition became transmuted into managed competition: a semantic change which recognized that health authorities were more concerned to establish long-term relationships with providers than to engage in promiscuous one-night stands with whoever offered the best bargain. Increasingly purchasing became another name for planning (Redmayne 1995). The scope of GP fundholding was extended. The new policy emphasis on population health outcomes, heralded by *The Health of the Nation*, had to be accommodated. So, too, had a new strategy for community services. The implementation of the new capitation formula meant that some districts faced massive budget cuts.

The pains of transformation were, temporarily at least, eased by the fact that the government was prepared to pour extra funds into the NHS in the early 1990s in order to make a success of its reforms. But the burden of bringing about the transformation meant that the first priority for those engaged in running the NHS was survival in a turbulent environment: to avoid being crushed by the demands on them. In other words, administrative and managerial resources were largely absorbed by the need to keep the machinery running even while redesigning it. Changing priorities in the allocation of resources inevitably, therefore, was not on the top of the agenda, although it began to creep up it as the 1990s progressed.

The point emerges clearly if we examine the annual guidance on priorities sent out by the NHS Management Executive, the branch of the Department of Health responsible for the implementation of policy (which, in 1995, was to be relabelled the NHS Executive and to take over responsibility for policy as well). The first to be issued after the introduction of the reforms (NHS Management Executive 1991) included the following guidance to regional managers for transmission through the service. Health authorities were expected:

- to set targets for improvements in health outcomes, in line with *The Health of the Nation*;
- to develop community care plans;
- to deliver further reductions in waiting times;
- to include 'challenging but realistic' quality standards in contracts;
- to start moving towards basing district health authority budgets on the weighted capitation formula;

- to ensure that cash limits were not exceeded;
- to monitor the prescribing budgets of GPs;
- to demonstrate that resources were being used more efficiently and to increase the volume of services being delivered;
- to achieve the Department's targets for reducing the hours worked by doctors in training;
- to ensure that districts produced purchasing plans.

These are only the highlights of the 1991 guidance. The list would have had to be much longer to be exhaustive. But the highlights are sufficient to indicate the shift in the definition of what was meant by 'priorities' that had taken place since the documents of the 1970s discussed in the previous chapter. These are administrative, not resource, priorities. Significantly, the sections dealing with purchasing plans had nothing to say about the direction of desired change – about whether or not there should be a shift in the distribution of resources between competing sectors and services – but were chiefly concerned with processes and format. So, for example, health authorities were exhorted to consult providers and clinicians about proposed changes and to ensure that any such changes would 'benefit local people and have the support of local GPs'. Similarly, as far as contents were concerned, districts were advised that purchasing plans should 'summarise the key benefits the purchaser is looking to secure for local people' and set out their approach to quality and efficiency improvements.

The character of the annual circular of guidance did not change greatly in the following years, although the contents varied from year to year. The 1992 circular (NHS Management Executive 1992) saw the 'overriding aim' as being 'to make improved health the focus of all our efforts in health promotion, illness prevention, treatment, rehabilitation and prevention of impairment and disability'. To achieve this, health authorities were instructed to 'embrace a wider role as champions for health in the local community', 'develop strong alliances with other agencies', 'invest in primary and community care, and ensure a better balance between hospital and community services' and 'set an example as healthy employers'. But in addition to this 'overriding aim', ministers also set 'three top priorities': implementing *The Health of the Nation Strategy*, ensuring high quality health and social care in the community and implementing the *Patient's Charter* standards. And, as if that were not enough, health authorities were also to carry out 'organisational change and staff development' and improve their machinery of financial control.

Most of these themes reappeared in the following year's circular (NHS Management Executive 1993). This, however, expanded the detail and added some new requirements. So, for example, health authorities were exhorted to ensure that there were adequate services for people from ethnic minorities, that day surgery should continue to increase and that internal communication strategies should be developed. Above all, there was more emphasis on 'achieving greater efficiency and effectiveness through our use of resources and organisational development'.

The 1994 document (NHS Management Executive 1994) acknowledged that 'any exercise in setting priorities becomes devalued if it simply includes everything we would like to do', but still set health authorities a searching examination paper. Not only were most of the previous themes continued. In addition the circular set out the 'success criteria' for 1995/6, against which the performance of health authorities was to be measured. These included meeting *Patient's Charter* standards, greater patient satisfaction with the NHS complaints machinery, a demonstrable input by local people into key decisions by purchasers, developing local pay determination and exploiting the potential of the Private Finance Initiative.

The 1994 circular was notable also for giving the clearest and most emphatic expression yet to the Department of Health's growing enthusiasm for 'knowledge based medicine'. Driving the department's enthusiasm was a simple assumption. If only scientific evidence could be used to identify those procedures and forms of treatment which did not appear to be effective, then resources would be freed for those services which promised to deliver greater 'health gains' (a favourite phrase in the departmental vocabulary of the 1990s). New demands would be met by liquidating existing commitments rather than requiring extra resources. Science would dissolve – or at least mitigate – the dilemmas of choosing between competing claims. Accordingly, the Department of Health invested heavily in a research programme into clinical effectiveness and a dissemination strategy for making relevant information available to health authorities and clinicians. But while there had been much generalized exhortation directed at health authorities in earlier years, the 1994 circular translated rhetoric into very specific requirements. Health authorities were instructed to increase investment in 1995/6 'in at least two interventions known to be effective' and to reduce investment 'in at least two interventions which have been identified as less effective'.

The 1995 circular (NHS Executive 1995) marked further progress towards turning what had started out as a shopping list of desirable policy aims into a hierarchy of priorities, with less emphasis on detail. It also put immediate priorities into a wider context. Overall, the performance of the NHS was to be judged by its progress in meeting three objectives: equity, efficiency and responsiveness to the needs of individual patients. The list of priorities nevertheless remained formidable. There was the familiar emphasis on improving the cost effectiveness of services, ensuring that 'integrated services are in place . . . to allow elderly, disabled or vulnerable people to be supported in the community' and giving 'greater voice and influence to users of NHS services'. In addition, the 1994 circular developed fortissimo a theme which had previously only emerged pianissimo: health authorities were to work towards 'the development of a primary care-led NHS'.

Two features of these circulars need to be noted before we turn to the ways in which health authorities took their decisions about priorities in the allocation of resources. First, the evolution of the circulars can be seen as at least a partial response to the criticism that health authorities were suffering from priority overload: progress from promiscuity to relative parsimony in the production of priorities. But even in their slimmed down version, the priorities still presented health authorities with a crowded agenda and were calculated to induce a collective nervous breakdown in any authority which attempted to deal with all of them. Second, the circulars from the centre, for all their specificity on so many points, did not provide any guidance about the distribution of resources between services. In this respect, they were very different from the priority documents of the 1970s. The difference is, of course, explicable in terms of the switch of emphasis in public policy from inputs to outputs, noted in the previous chapter. If the performance of health authorities was to be judged by their ability to bring about specific outputs – and, more important still, outcomes measured in terms of the impact on the population's health – why not leave it to them to determine the most appropriate balance in the use of resources? Accordingly, health authorities were largely left to make their own interpretation of the government's priorities when making their decisions about how to divide up their budget between competing claims.

This conclusion is reinforced when we look at the most conspicuous example of the government having a very clear priority in the allocation of resources and providing ring-fenced funds from the centre for a specific purpose: the funds allocated to regional health authorities to deal with a new problem, AIDS. The allocations were based on a formula that weighted populations by the incidence of HIV and AIDS. But within these ring-fenced budgets – which could not be diverted to other uses – regions used resources very differently (Craven *et al.* 1994), in part because the allocation formula did not adequately reflect the very different pressures on them. So, for example, in 1991/2 the treatment cost per case varied by a factor of four. Similarly, the regions and their districts differed greatly in how they spent the money allocated to prevention: some directed their efforts at the high-risk categories in the population while others launched all-embracing campaigns directed at just about everyone, including children.

In examining the purchasing priorities of health authorities in the next section, we therefore start with the expectation that variations will be the norm. And that is precisely what we find: a mixture of convergence in terms of rhetoric and process (reflecting the vocabulary of central government exhortation) and continued divergence in the practice of resource distribution (reflecting local capacities and circumstances).

PURCHASER PRIORITIES

In this section we draw on the results of four surveys carried out at the Centre for the Analysis of Social Policy at the University of Bath between 1992 and 1996 (Klein and Redmayne 1992; Redmayne *et al.* 1993; Redmayne 1995, 1996). In each year, all health authorities were asked to supply their purchasing plans; in addition, in 1995 they were asked for their five-year strategic plans. The number of authorities approached varied from year to year, as amalgamations changed the configuration of the NHS. So, too, did the response rate, which ranged from about 60 to 90 per cent. In interpreting the evidence of these surveys, we draw, in addition, on interviews carried out with both executive and non-executive members of health authorities in ten case study areas, chosen to illustrate a wide range of circumstances. The case studies represented a wide geographical spread of health authorities operating in very different contexts, ranging from deprived inner cities to more affluent semi-rural areas. They also included authorities both gaining and losing funding in consequence of the implementation of the weighted capitation formulae and therefore facing very different financial pressures.

The most obvious characteristic of the purchasing documents, as of the strategy documents, is the sheer variety of their presentation. Anyone coming to them in the hope of being able to compare systematically where the money goes, and how the distribution of funds between competing services is planned to change, is likely to be disappointed. Any statement of priorities would, it might be thought, take as its starting point the existing configuration of services and provision, how these compared with other health authorities and the evidence about local shortfalls. Very few purchasing plans provide such base line information. The next step, again it might be thought, would be to indicate the implications for the distribution of resources of any policy decisions taken about priorities. Again, however, only a minority of plans provide such information. Changes in the financial commitments have usually to be winkled out from a mass of statistics about contracts with different providers. Analysing the plans is therefore an exercise in tin-opening, and some of the tins turn out to be extremely resistant to efforts to prise out information from them.

There are exceptions. Some of the plans are more comprehensive and explicit than others. And some kinds of information are more available than others: in particular, purchasers have become more open about what they will not buy, a point which will be explored further in the next chapter, which turns from priority setting to rationing. And, over the years, the presentation has improved. Overall, however, there is still a long way to go before the hope that the 1991 reforms would force health authorities to be transparent about the distributional consequences of their choices is realized.

All this is not to suggest that the health authorities do not make priority decisions. They do. In particular, they do so at the level of verbal commitment: priority talk is cheap. Most purchasing plans contain long lists of priorities. But there is a large gap between the aspirational priorities, i.e. what the authorities would like to do, and the financial commitments actually made. The point is illustrated by Tables 5.1 and 5.2, drawn from the 1993 survey. Table 5.1 shows the ten priorities which got the most frequent mentions. Table 5.2 shows the distribution of expenditure on different services for which money was actually allocated by those authorities that gave sufficient details in their plans for the sums to be calculated. There is little relationship between the two. So, for example, while mental health was mentioned by more health authorities among their top ten priorities than any other issue, in

Table 5.1   Aspirational priorities, 1993/4: the top ten priorities
mentioned most frequently by purchasers

Service	No. of purchasers mentioning the service as a priority (n = 100)
Mental health	74
Heart disease	56
Learning difficulties	54
Cancer	54
Community services	51
Children	51
Maternity	49
Accident prevention	49
HIV/AIDS	49
Elderly	48

Source: Redmayne *et al.* (1993).

Table 5.2   Distribution of priority expenditure, 1993/4

Service	Amount (£ million)	Proportion of total (per cent)
Acute	35.5	58
Community	10.6	17
Other (miscellaneous)	6.8	11
Mental health	4.9	8
Elderly	2.6	4
Learning difficulties	1.3	2

Source: Redmayne *et al.* (1993).

fact only 17 per cent of the expenditure allocated for priority
developments was allocated to this service. In contrast, acute
services received 58 per cent of all the money allocated, even
though they did not feature in the aspirational priorities to anything
like the same extent as mental health. Even when health authorities
did put money behind their priorities, the amounts were often very
small and, in some cases, appeared to be symbolic gestures. Overall, there was little sign that the rhetorical commitment to giving
priority to community and primary care services, at the expense of
the hospital sector, was being translated into equivalent resource
commitments.

The commitment, however, remains. Most of the five-year strategy plans of health authorities, analysed in the 1994 survey, tended to echo the Department of Health's guidance in the emphasis on developing a primary care led NHS and transferring activity from hospitals to the community. In this respect, at least, there was a surprising degree of unanimity. It remains to be seen how far this commitment will be translated into practice given the unresolved tension between the government's own policy priorities; in particular, between cutting waiting times and lists, which may mean giving priority to funding the acute services, *and* developing primary and community care.

But, it is important to note, health authorities – assuming that they carry out their strategic plans for reconfiguring services – will continue to vary greatly in their expenditure patterns. Only a few authorities provide details about the resource implications of their strategic plans. Those that do so, however, show great variations in the distribution of funds to different services: the proportion of the total budget to be allocated to acute services at the end of the decade ranges from 36 to 58 per cent, while the range for mental health service is from 4.5 to 13.8 per cent. These figures are difficult to interpret. They may reflect differences in accounting practices. They may reflect differences in local circumstances. They may reflect different historical inheritances. They may reflect differences in the priorities. The strategic plans do not provide the information required to come to any definitive interpretation: a conclusion which, in itself, may be significant if it is assumed that the choices and policies of health authorities should be transparent and comprehensible. In any case, there is little sign of convergence.

Nor does the picture improve if we consider outputs rather than inputs. Indeed, it becomes even more opaque. The strategic plans only rarely translate their priorities into what these will imply for access to, and the availability of, specific services to the population. Neither does it help if we take one step further and move to outcomes. Health authorities have indeed adopted wholesale *Health of the Nation* targets for improvements in the population's health and included them in their priorities. Policies of prevention are stressed. But, again, this is difficult to interpret. Many of the targets have little to do with the activities of the NHS and everything to do with socio-economic conditions. Further, many of the targets themselves appear to be – to a large extent – extrapolations of past trends. Embracing the *Health of the Nation* targets as a priority may therefore often be a relatively cheap way for health authorities to follow departmental guidance.

The direct influence of central government guidance is also evident in the way in which health authorities set about preparing their purchasing plans. They do indeed consult general practitioners, as they have been exhorted to do. Similarly, they consult – if to a lesser degree – the public in a variety of ways. It is not clear how much influence such consultation exercises have over the decisions taken about priorities. The evidence suggests that while the views of GPs carry very considerable weight in shaping priorities, if only because health authorities need the active cooperation of GPs, public consultation tends to be used to legitimize decisions already taken, if only because such consultation often yields only ambiguous or conflicting results, a point to which we return in Chapter 10. The government's priorities for shaping the processes by which health authorities produce their purchasing plans appear to have been largely achieved.

The Department of Health's influence on the way in which health authorities tackle priorities cuts deeper still, however. Most of these priorities, as we saw in the first half of this chapter, had little or nothing to do with the distribution of funds between services or choices between different claims on resources: while ministers were always prompt to include any issue that had caught the headlines in their list of priorities – such as care in the community for the mentally ill – they carefully avoided putting any price tag on their guidance, leaving it to health authorities to find the money. The advice flowing out of the department, via the Management Executive, was predominantly about achieving greater efficiency and effectiveness, on the one hand, and about managerial and administrative developments, on the other. And this emphasis is clearly reflected in the priorities of health authorities. Much of their activity, as reflected in the purchasing plans, was dominated by negotiating contracts with providers that cut prices and increased output and implementing the various administrative changes that flowed from the NHS's continuing evolution. Simply keeping the machine running, learning how to cope with the new situation created by the purchaser–provider split and reacting to immediate national and local pressures strained the capacities of health authorities.

If the impact of the 1991 NHS reforms on resource allocation policies therefore appears to have been disappointingly small, it was in part at least because health authorities had many other, immediately pressing preoccupations and demands on their managerial resources. But the rather unflattering broad brush conclusions that we have presented so far, which suggest that little changed in the post-reform NHS, become modified if we adopt a rather different perspective and examine the fine print of health authority activity. Setting priorities, as we shall see in the next section, is a highly problematic activity: making choices is not easy.

THE PROBLEMS OF CHOOSING

If we wanted to construct an ideal model for decision-making about priorities by health authorities, what would it look like? Following the synoptic model of rational decision-making, it might be expected to have the following four elements (Klein *et al.* 1995):

1 The purchaser has to draw up an inventory of existing service provision: that is, there has to be a benchmark picture of what the authority's money is currently buying and for whom.
2 The purchaser has to assemble the evidence about unmet need or frustrated demand in order to establish in what respects, and to what extent, existing provision falls short of what should be available to the population.
3 The purchaser has to develop a currency of evaluation for assessing both existing commitments and new claims on resources.
4 The purchaser has to compare the competing claims on resources according to the criteria already determined in order to determine spending priorities. Crucially, if benefits (however measured) are to be maximized, existing commitments must be treated exactly like new candidates for spending.

The purchasing plans, as we have seen, tend to be conspicuous for their failure to include these elements. But it cannot be assumed that this is necessarily evidence of original sin. It may simply reflect the fact that the model makes unrealistic demands: that the concepts and tools needed to translate it into action still have to be developed. In what follows we therefore take the different components of the model and examine the extent to which health authorities could be expected to follow its requirements.

Consider, first, the problem of information about existing activities. The NHS has, historically, been an information-poor organization, in terms of both the scope and the quality of the data that are available. As the chairman of one health authority, an industrialist, reported with a sense of disbelief: 'no one knows how much anything costs in the NHS'. And although the 1991 reforms prompted a major investment in information technology, they also exposed a new problem: that of information asymmetry between purchasers and providers. Quite simply, providers knew much more about what was happening than purchasers. As one health authority chief executive put it in an interview, 'When purchasing started, it was rather like going into a supermarket with a trolley and asking the staff to fill it.' Thus health authorities are only gradually filling in the base line picture of what services they are actually providing, at what cost and to whom. The extent to which they have done so varies greatly, but at least the success of a minority shows that this problem is surmountable.

The problem of collecting systematic evidence about unmet need or frustrated demand, and identifying the implications for the distribution of NHS resources, is perhaps more intractable. The principle of 'needs assessment' tends to be much invoked: it is an essential part of the post–1991 NHS vocabulary. But there are very real difficulties about applying it in practice (Stevens and Gabbay 1991). Not only is the concept of 'need', as argued earlier, ambiguous. Definitions of need tend to change over time; moreover, to diagnose a 'need' is to prompt the question of 'a need for what?' So, for example, information about a population's morbidity does not necessarily tell us anything about what mix or permutation of services is appropriate in response. Difficulties are further compounded because 'needs' may be defined rather differently by NHS professionals and the public: while the former may define them in terms of what is technically effective, the latter may define them in terms of accessibility.

The last point underlines the difficulty of devising a currency of evaluation for assessing different services. Whose criteria should they be? And what if the criteria conflict? Should equity in the distribution of resources – i.e. making services equally accessible to all sections of the population – trump efficiency? The former may indicate spreading out resources; the latter may suggest concentrating resources in specialized centres. Should the criteria be driven by utilitarian analysis or by other values? Similarly, what if the aim of maximizing the population's health conflicts with improving the health of the most deprived sections of the population?

The doubts raised about the feasibility of adopting the synoptic model of decision making apply, of course, with even greater force to the fourth element: a systematic comparison of the benefits yielded by existing services and the benefits that would be yielded by investments in new services. Even if the various questions about assessing need and devising a currency of evaluation could be resolved at some future time – an issue to which we return, in greater depth, in Chapter 8 – it is clear that a systematic comparison of the benefits yielded by all existing services and all possible potential services is well beyond the capacity of health authorities at present. Much of the information that would be required for such an exercise simply does not exist at present. So even if we knew how 'benefits' are to be measured, health authorities are in no position to take such an over-arching view.

Nor does the notion of 'health gains', much invoked in purchasing plans, help much in this respect. In practice, we found that health authorities tend to use this concept as a way of forcing providers to be explicit about what improvements would follow from any investment, rather than as a means of summing up such improvements on a common scale. 'Health gains' are non-convertible currencies. Moreover, they do not provide purchasers with independent criteria. As one purchaser put it, 'We have to rely on clinicians to tell us about health gains. We are not in a position to make those kinds of judgements.'

It is the excessive and unrealistic requirements of the synoptic, rational decision-making model, rather than the shortcomings of health authorities, which therefore explain our findings about resource priorities. There have been no dramatic shifts or changes, and priority creep has been the norm, because health authorities responded to uncertainty and lack of information by adopting strategies of incremental adaptation. Some authorities did carry out experiments in which their executives and non-executives sought both to develop criteria for weighting different claims on resources and to rank different health services accordingly (Cochrane *et al.* 1991). But these served largely to illuminate the problems involved rather than to solve them. Formal rankings of priorities, according to agreed criteria, remain the exception rather than the rule. 'We now know how to prioritize mounds of paper but not yet how to prioritize health services' was the conclusion of one non-executive.

Instead, rather than reviewing and revising their priorities across the board, most health authorities broke up the problem into more manageable segments (see, for example, Ham *et al.* 1993). They tended to review services within existing resource envelopes: purchasing is about 'tinkering at the edges', as one executive put it. They devolved the information gathering task by setting up working parties to review services within those envelopes. The emphasis was, in short, as much on changing the way in which resources were used as on shifting resources from one service to another. Contracting was used to promote new priorities in the use, rather than the distribution, of resources. In particular, many authorities devoted much energy to prompting clinicians to develop protocols designed to promote more efficient and effective practices.

Our interviews showed that there was some frustration about this 'tinkering' approach, particularly among non-executives new to the culture of the NHS. They were puzzled by the assumption that the greater part of their authority's resources were already committed and therefore could not be questioned or shifted. As one of them put it, 'We spend a lot of time talking about how to use our incremental funds, which are proportionately very little, and we ignore the "historical baggage" which is the largest part of the NHS and its resources. We have not got around to talking about or planning for 90 per cent of the organization.'

Over time, as the newcomers to the NHS gather confidence, the assumption that the bulk of existing commitments is beyond scrutiny will therefore come under increasing challenge. Already, practices vary. Health authorities facing budget cuts under the weighted capitation formula inevitably tended to be more radical than those which gained and could, as a result, achieve a new pattern of resource distribution by adopting a policy of differential growth. Some authorities adopted the practice of announcing their priorities for new developments and invited providers to bid for funds, so in effect putting the burden of demonstrating the benefits yielded by any investment on the latter. Others invited bids and then ranked them according to predetermined criteria.

In the City and Hackney Health Authority, for example, one point was awarded if the proposal had been prioritized by the Community Health Council or by GPs, a further point was awarded if it contributed to the promotion of equity, up to two points were awarded if there was evidence about enhanced effectiveness or efficiency and up to three points were awarded if the proposal promoted collaboration with primary care and for its implementability. The effectiveness criterion proved to be particularly difficult to apply and most proposals scored nil under this heading. The reason, as explained by the authority's Director of Public Health, was: 'There is much rhetoric about only investing in cost-effective services. However there is little evidence about the cost-effectiveness of specific projects, so that to follow the rhetoric would mean disbanding and ceasing to purchase about 80% of health services'

(Jacobson 1994), a central point to which we shall return when considering the question of whether promoting knowledge based medicine can obviate the need for rationing.

Other authorities tried different techniques. Southampton experimented with a simulation exercise designed to test the claims of different services (Heginbotham 1992). Wandsworth was among those which attempted to rank different types of services in order of priority. Interestingly (and in line with the rule of rescue), top of the list came treatments that prevent death and allow a full or partial recovery, followed by prevention, maternity and treatment for acute or chronic conditions where one treatment improves the quality of life, with fertility problems coming near the bottom. Mostly, though, authorities tended to avoid explicit ranking exercises. Instead they used multiple and very heterogeneous criteria in assessing different claims on resources. These included better outcomes, value for money, improving the accessibility or acceptability of services, provider pressure, the number of people likely to benefit, the potential impact on morbidity and mortality and the feasibility of making the necessary changes.

This last criterion underlines a further constraint on health authorities in moving resources between services: the implementability of priorities. Considerations of organizational feasibility often inhibit radical shifts in the short term. Most important, existing services tend to have ready-made constituencies of support: most conspicuously, proposals for hospital closures tend to mobilize coalitions of providers and users in opposition. Conversely, new services – by definition – tend to have only a potential constituency. The former, moreover, is concentrated, while the latter is diffuse (Marmor 1983). As one purchaser put it, 'There is a lot of support for the status quo and the providers always seem to be several steps ahead of purchasers in rallying the support of the press and the local community to stop any changes'.

It is therefore not surprising that health authorities tend to be cautiously incremental. They may be clear about their long-term priorities, as their strategy documents suggest, but they are moving towards them using a strategy of 'purposeful opportunism' (Klein and O'Higgins 1985) – that is, exploiting opportunities as they arise in moving towards their chosen aims. The need for caution is further reinforced by another consideration. In those parts of the country where there is no effective competition, purchasers have to rely on persuasion – rather than the often empty threat of shifting their custom – to prod providers into shifting resources between specialties or services. In the words of one non-executive, 'There is a very good reason for avoiding dramatic changes. It means we can also avoid the confrontations that usually accompany dramatic methods. We want to keep the providers non-hostile while at the same time getting them to do things our way.'

Our finding that priority setting in the post-1991 era has not, as yet, brought about any radical redistribution of resources between services should not come as a surprise. The focus of change, to recapitulate, has been on change within services. Accordingly, in the next chapter we move from examining priority setting to rationing in the narrower sense – from macro decisions to micro decisions – and turn to looking at the effects of decisions by health authorities on who gets what in the way of services.

6

LIFTING THE VEILS
FROM RATIONING?

One of the features of the 1990s debate about managing scarce resources in the NHS is that while everyone is keen to talk about priorities, there is a conspicuous reluctance to talk about rationing. Priority talk suggests boldness in making tough choices; rationing talk suggests inadequacy of provision. Priorities are what ministers boast of; rationing is what opposition politicians accuse them of (see, for example, Parliamentary Debates 1995). For while setting priorities may imply rationing, it does not make the consequences of the resource allocation decisions transparent. The semantic conventions of the debate can therefore be seen as yet another version of the strategy for centralizing credit while diffusing blame: hence its appeal for both ministers and health authorities.

There is, in addition, a genuine difficulty about linking decisions about resource allocations to the impact on service delivery. The relationship may be complex and difficult to predict. If a particular service is given low priority in funding by a health authority, this may well mean that the providers concerned will operate under more stringent budgetary constraints. But how providers react to such constraints is an open question. They may use available resources more efficiently, thereby closing any gap between supply and demand. Alternatively, they may adopt any (or all) of the strategies in the rationing repertoire, such as deflection, dilution or denial. This is why looking simply at the decisions taken by health authorities about priorities in the allocation of resources – as we did in the previous chapter – tells us little about the implications for the availability, or otherwise, of services for the public. The practice of rationing at the point of service delivery remains veiled. In effect, health authorities are able to distance themselves from

Table 6.1 Variations between health authorities in carrying out selected standard procedures

Procedure	Minimum rate	Maximum rate	Bottom 10 per cent	Top 10 per cent
Cataract surgery	149	469	201	363
Coronary artery by-pass graft	0.5	59	5	42
Hip replacement	36	152	51	110
Knee replacement	18	86	29	64
Tonsillectomy	8	403	102	263

Finished consultant episodes: rates per 100,000 resident population, unstandardized.
Source: Department of Health, *Health Service Indicators, 1993–4.*

the consequences of their decisions, which tend to be diffuse, difficult to identify with any precision and lacking in visibility.

In some cases, however, the veil has been lifted, if only partially and tentatively, as health authorities have begun to address the issue of rationing (in the strict sense) by taking decisions about which services *not* to buy. It is these experiments in stripping off the veils that are the subject of this chapter: as we shall see, the threat of all being revealed has in many cases led to a rapid retreat to the traditional strategy of sheltering behind the fig leaf of clinical discretion. But before we explore this topic further, it is important to note that non-decisions are as important as decisions. In other words, the implications of maintaining the status quo may be as significant as decisions to change it. Indeed, they may be more important, given that, as we shall see, most of the explicit rationing decisions tend to be at the margin of service delivery.

The point can be simply illustrated. Health authorities, as already noted, vary greatly in the services that they make available to their populations. Thus variations in the rate of performing certain standard procedures have been both gross and persistent throughout the history of the NHS, and cannot be explained by differences in the demography of the population (Ham 1988). And they have persisted in the 1990s. The point is illustrated by Table 6.1, which shows the variations between health authorities in the rates of performing five standard procedures. So, for example, rates for coronary artery bypass graft surgery varied by a factor of over 100 between different health authorities and rates for hip replacements varied by a factor of almost five.

Some of these figures may well be statistical flukes. The variations become less dramatic if we ignore the statistical outliers and compare the top 10 per cent with the bottom 10 per cent of health authorities. They are still very considerable, however: the rates for coronary artery bypass graft surgery still vary by a factor of eight and those for hip replacements by a factor of two. Some, too, might be explained by differences in the composition of the population. In the case of some procedures, notably tonsillectomy, it may be that high rates reflect over-zealous practices. Even so, it is difficult to resist the general conclusion that low rates probably (though not certainly) reflect a form of implicit rationing, with both general practitioners and the population having been conditioned over the years to expect and demand a lower level of service than in other parts of the country.

Rationing, in short, may be most acceptable when it is not perceived as such: when it represents not so much a consciously taken decision to deliver less than the best but a local culture where medical aspirations and public expectations reinforce each other in not asking too much of the NHS or demanding miracles from medical science. Lack of supply creates its own lack of demand. Where there were no consultants generating work for their specialisms, there were no patients. It is thus the lottery of history which, to a large extent, still determines who gets what. And it is this largely invisible form of rationing – and therefore unresented, unless translated into long waiting lists – which provides the context for the explicit, and therefore more controversial, decisions taken by some health authorities to limit the NHS menu of available services, to which we now turn.

LIMITING THE NHS MENU

The process by which health authorities have moved towards limiting their shopping lists – and therefore the availability of services on the NHS menu – has resembled a complex dance of the veils, teasing the viewer with a glimpse of bold decision-making which is then quickly wrapped up again. For the story revealed by the successive surveys of purchasing plans is, to anticipate our findings, simple: a retreat to the NHS's traditional reliance on clinicians to decide who gets what. It begins with a small minority of

Table 6.2 Limiting the menu (1992–3 purchasing plans)

Services	Number of health authorities
Tattoo removal	7
GIFT/IVF	6
Reversal of sterilization/vasectomy	4
General cosmetic surgery	4
Adult bat ears	3
Breast augmentation	3
Cosmetic rhinoplasty	3
Removal of non-genital warts	2
Cosmetic varicose veins	1
Homeopathy	1
Sex change operation	1
Multi-allergy syndrome	1
Liposuction/lipectomy	1
Mastopexy	1
Repair of nipple	1
Buttock lift	1
Blepharoplasty	1

Source: Klein and Redmayne (1992).

health authorities boldly announcing that they would cease purchasing certain procedures. It ends with an increasing number of
health authorities announcing restrictions on what they propose to
buy on behalf of their populations, but usually qualifying their
decisions with escape clauses designed to put the ultimate responsibility for determining the selection and treatment of individual
patients on doctors. When health authorities decide to exclude
certain procedures from their shopping lists, or to limit the funds
available, they are increasingly putting the onus on clinicians to
make out a case for treating specific patients.

In the first wave of purchasing plans analysed, 12 out of the 114
health authorities stated that they would either deny or limit the
availability of specific forms of treatment (Klein and Redmayne
1992). Table 6.2 sets out the list of the procedures involved. The list
is interesting for a number of reasons. It underlines that explicit
rationing by denial was taking place very much at the margins of
NHS activity. The procedures concerned represent the small
change of NHS expenditure. No one has ever suggested that, for
example, removing tattoos or lifting buttocks represents a major

drain on NHS resources. And while treatment for infertility involves rather larger sums, it still represents only a minor investment of NHS funds.

Further, the list indicates the way in which the health authorities were, if only implicitly and unconsciously, redefining the limits of the health care system's responsibilities. The conditions listed fall into two categories. First, there are those which can be argued to be self-inflicted (like tattoos), where, therefore, those concerned should be responsible for remedying the consequences of their own actions. Second, there are other conditions where the case for intervention appears to rest on need as defined not by the medical profession but by the patient, as in the case of cosmetic procedures, where again it can be argued that responsibility should fall on the person concerned.

In short, the list suggests that the criteria used for making judgements about whether or not to buy these procedures were rather different from those usually invoked. For the criterion used seems to have been not so much whether the procedures were technically effective but whether they represented activities appropriate for a publicly funded health care system. No one has argued that tattoo removal is ineffective in that it fails to deal with the disfigurement or that buttock lift is ineffective in that it fails to bring about the desired outcome. Rather, the implicit question appears to have been that even if such procedures brought about a health gain – inasmuch as they improved well-being and capacity for social functioning of those concerned – was it the responsibility of the NHS to pay for them?

We shall return to this question later in this chapter, when we examine in rather more detail the specific issues raised by in vitro fertilization (IVF). For the time being, however, it is sufficient to note that to put this question is, once again, to underline the ambiguity and slipperiness of the concept of health gains when deciding purchasing policies. After all, there are a great many interventions which may produce health gains in the sense of improved well-being and capacity for social functioning – for example, providing good housing – but which are thought to be outside the NHS's competence. So the concept provides a somewhat elastic tool for defining the frontiers of the NHS's responsibilities.

Neither the number of authorities committing themselves to explicit rationing by denial, nor the conditions concerned, changed greatly in the two years that followed. The 1993 survey of purchasing plans (Redmayne *et al.* 1993) showed a fall in the numbers, from 12 to four. The 1994 survey (Redmayne 1995) showed a recovery to 11. The list of procedures covered expanded but did not change greatly in character. So, for example, the 1994–5 purchasing plans included – in addition to the items in Table 6.2 – residential psychotherapy and screening for prostate cancer. Each of these was listed by only one authority. More significant perhaps – because it involved a procedure that is more in the mainstream of NHS activity – was the decision by four authorities not to purchase treatment for varicose veins.

What did change greatly, however, were the tactics adopted by health authorities in their endeavour to limit their purchasing commitments. Outright, explicit denial risked provoking opposition, not only from potential beneficiaries but (much more importantly) from the medical profession. For doctors, a decision not to purchase a particular procedure represented a challenge to clinical autonomy. Health authorities appeared to be arrogating to themselves the right to decide who should be treated and how: the traditional preserve of the medical profession. This, clearly, was something that had to be fought. Doctors were quick to point out that the case for carrying out specific procedures depended on the particular circumstances of individual patients: that even tattoo removal or gender reassignment could be justified if it meant that the person concerned could, as a result, be enabled to lead a normal life.

Instead of limiting the NHS menu, therefore, health authorities increasingly turned to specifying the conditions of eligibility for treatment in cooperation with the medical profession. In effect, the criteria were re-medicalized. As one purchaser argued:

> The general philosophy adopted locally is to build on clinical decision-making rather than simplistically exclude lists of procedures. It is clear that, within a single diagnostic category which may superficially seem easy to delete, there will be patients for whom NHS treatment is justified – for example, an individual with a tattoo that is affecting their ability to work should be treated.

Accordingly, the emphasis switched to negotiating guidelines and protocols with local clinicians. It would be the clinicians, albeit prompted by the health authorities, who would define the conditions under which treatment would be offered. While the purchasers would determine the constraints under which specific services operated, clinicians would continue to decide how the resources would be used. In short, the traditional division of responsibility within the NHS was maintained. In one respect, however, the new era of guidelines and protocols marked a break with the past. Whereas in the past decisions about appropriateness and effectiveness had been taken by individual clinicians, often extremely idiosyncratically, they were now to be taken by the clinicians collectively on the basis of scientific evidence in line with the new faith in knowledge based medicine. Or so, at any rate, ran the theory.

This, then, was the pattern in the first half of the 1990s. A shift of emphasis is apparent, however, in the purchasing plans produced in 1995 (Redmayne 1996). The number of health authorities excluding specific procedures from their 1995–6 shopping lists increased to 23 and the number planning to make exclusions in 1996–7 rose to 26. As before, however, the exclusions were not absolute: the door was left open for the treatments to be carried out if there were persuasive clinical reasons for doing so. Further, the number of procedures specified also increased considerably: the complete list is given in the Appendix. The multiplication of exclusions reflected largely the unpackaging of generic categories. Instead of excluding 'cosmetic surgery' as a general category, health authorities listed a larger number of specific procedures under this general heading: for example, removing adult birthmarks, abdominoplasty and so on.

Although the number of these exclusions has increased, their character has not. They are still, overwhelmingly, procedures at the margins of NHS activity. And their exclusion seems to reflect the belief that the procedures involved do not deal with medical need in the strict sense but, rather, are a response to the social and psychological wants of those seeking treatment. However, this conclusion must be qualified in one important respect. The 1995 plans put more stress than their predecessors on evidence about effectiveness as a criterion for purchasing, very much in line with the guidance on priorities from the NHS Executive. Among the excluded procedures listed are mass cholesterol screening for low risk people, dilation and curettage for women under 40 and grommets for glue ear in children (about which more below). And even when such procedures are not excluded from the shopping lists, health authorities frequently announce their intention of cutting the budgets allocated for purchasing them because of doubts about their effectiveness: what is delicately if inelegantly termed 'disinvestment'.

The purchasing plans are also cautious about committing themselves to funding expensive new drug treatments. The example of interferon beta–1b is a case in point. This is a new drug for the treatment of multiple sclerosis, at an estimated cost of about £10,000 a year per patient (Walley and Barton 1995). Some health authorities are refusing to fund it, because they believe that its effectiveness remains to be demonstrated; others are proposing to draw up guidelines to control its use.

The first phase of purchasing in the post-1991 era thus ended in a partial retreat from explicit rationing by exclusion. The veil of clinical judgement had proved too useful to discard. Instead most health authorities, in cooperation with the clinicians, adopted a modified form of the strategy. Services and procedures would not be struck off the NHS menu but given low priority in resource allocation. And within restricted resource envelopes, clinicians would decide whom to treat, and how, according to their own criteria of appropriateness. Science, it seems, had come to the rescue of scarcity, offering a new legitimation of selectivity. Patients would be turned away not because resources were scarce but because treatment would not be appropriate in their case. In the next section, we illustrate how this new emphasis – very much reflecting the priority guidelines from the centre, reviewed in the previous chapter – was expressed in the purchasing plans for the second half of the 1990s.

RATIONING BY SELECTIVITY

The high visibility and consequent contentiousness of the strategy of exclusion always meant, as we have seen, that it has only been used by a minority of health authorities and affected only rather marginal services. Conversely, the lower visibility of, and diffusion of responsibility involved in, a strategy of rationing by selection has meant that it has been used more widely. The trend has been to invoke evidence, drawn from medical or epidemiological research, that suggests that services or procedures previously provided as a matter of routine should be used more discriminatingly and selectively.

Consider, for example, the case of glue ear and grommets. Glue ear is a condition that affects the hearing of about 5 per cent of children between the ages of two and four at any one point in time. It is usually of short duration and resolved spontaneously. It is therefore not among the headline hitting health care problems, nor among the major claims on resources: the total cost of surgical intervention in the NHS is estimated to be about £30 million (approximately £300,000 a year per health authority, on average). But it features prominently in purchasing plans as a candidate for the more selective use of resources. The reason is that a report by a unit funded by the Department of Health to review and disseminate the results of research evidence (Effective Health Care 1992) showed that surgery for dealing with glue ear – in particular the insertion of grommets, at an average cost of about £300 – had tended to be carried out both too prematurely and too indiscriminately. On the basis of the available evidence, the report recommended the development of local protocols which would ensure a more selective use of surgery and a greater emphasis on 'watchful waiting'.

The recommendation has been taken up with some enthusiasm by health authorities. In one case, the purchaser 'intends to institute consultation with clinicians in primary and secondary care, and in the audiological services, to develop guidelines for a recognised system of care for children found to have glue ear. These should be drawn up so as to obviate unnecessary interventions, but so as to ensure that no child develops significant hearing impairments.' In another case, the purchasing plan reports that 'work will be undertaken with providers and GPs to ensure that surgical treatment of glue ear is limited to appropriate cases and that access to audiological services is sufficient to target procedures in this way.' In both cases, the aim is to restrict expenditure but to do so – as the language used demonstrates – by eliminating 'unnecessary' interventions and by limiting 'inappropriate' treatment. In both cases, too, this is to be achieved in cooperation with clinicians, since only they can decide in each individual case what is necessary or appropriate.

The example of glue ear and grommets has been examined at some length because it is representative of the kind of strategies used by health authorities in the second half of the 1990s to justify 'disinvestment' or exclusion. The same use of research evidence is apparent in the case of the two other examples of decisions to restrict spending given above: dilation and curettage for women under 40 and mass cholesterol screening for low-risk groups. In the former case, the guidance from the Royal College of Surgeons is that such operations should not be performed. In the latter case, there is no evidence that it prevents coronary heart disease.

Such decisions clearly limit access to the NHS in the sense that they restrict the menu of what is available. But they raise two questions. The first is how they will be implemented by clinicians, i.e. how individual doctors will interpret any guidelines or protocols in the case of individual patients. Are decisions about ineffectiveness or inappropriateness so clear cut that they are independent of the resource constraints under which clinicians work? The second is whether they can be described as rationing without distorting and stretching the meaning of the word to breaking point. If a given form of health care intervention is demonstrably, and self-evidently, ineffective or inappropriate, should the NHS be offering it in the first place? In such circumstances, is it not a misuse of the language to invoke the word 'rationing'? After all, we would not describe the NHS's refusal to allow snake oil to be prescribed as rationing. We shall have occasion to return to these questions in the chapters that follow. But we conclude this chapter by examining two case studies of rationing in the strictest and most visible sense, i.e. by denial, which raise some further issues.

THE CASE OF IN VITRO FERTILIZATION

IVF is one of a range of treatments for infertility. It involves surgically collected eggs and sperm being mixed together in the laboratory to fertilize under glass and subsequently being transferred to the uterus. It is effective in the sense that it results in live births in 40 per cent of cases having three cycles of treatment (Evans 1995), although the success rate varies both with the age of the women concerned and between different units carrying out the procedure. It is also expensive, because several attempts may have to be made before conception takes place: it has been estimated that the average cost per live birth is about £11,000 (Appleby 1993). This is considerably more than the cost per birth of other forms of fertility treatment. But for some women, those with blocked fallopian tubes, IVF is the treatment of last resort: if that is not offered, they will lose all hope of having a child. IVF therefore provides a case study in the allocation of resources to a procedure that is effective but expensive for the benefit of a self-defined minority group. Additionally, it highlights the problems involved in defining the boundaries of the NHS's responsibilities.

Health authorities are split as to whether or not to provide IVF on the NHS menu. In 1994 almost a quarter refused to purchase IVF (Wiles and Patel 1995). The reasons for refusing vary (Redmayne and Klein 1993). Some authorities take the view that since IVF is expensive, the money would be better spent elsewhere: one pointed out that for every cycle of IVF, which has a one in four chance of success, a new hip could be bought. Others argue that since IVF is available in the private sector of health care, people should pay for it themselves. Underlying all these responses appears to be the shared assumption that the NHS should not spend its money on – or at least give a high degree of priority to – people who are not seen to be 'ill'. Further, even those authorities which see the provision of fertility services as an important part of the NHS's responsibilities may refuse to buy IVF. In these cases, the argument is that resources should be used to organize their fertility services to maximize effectiveness rather than to fund the treatment of last resort.

The decision as to whether to buy IVF or not is affected by other considerations as well. The evidence suggests that decisions reflect as much the local balance of interests as the local balance of argument in different health authorities. In health authorities where there is a local consultant champion, and consequently a local constituency of support, the decision is likely to go in favour of purchasing IVF. Conversely, if there is no such local pressure from consultants, general practitioners and public, the decision is more likely to go the other way. Supply, in the case of IVF, generates demand.

But even those health authorities which decide to purchase IVF often do so on only a limited scale, in full awareness of the fact that this will mean rationing by selection. The strategy is to allocate a limited budget, usually leaving it to the clinicians involved to determine eligibility for treatment. Sometimes, however, the purchasers set out their own criteria. The most frequently invoked criterion is that of age: usually only women under 40 (sometimes under 35) will be considered for treatment, on the grounds that prospects for success diminish with age. Often, too, eligibility is limited to women who have no living children from their present or previous relationships. In a few cases, evidence of a stable relationship is also required. In other words, the criteria used appear to be a mix of 'capacity to benefit' (age), 'need' (no other children) and 'desert' (stable relationship).

Both the non-purchasers and the purchasers of IVF are therefore making judgements about complex issues that cannot be resolved by an appeal to science. Does the fact that medical intervention can remedy what is a deprivation for some people automatically translate it into a clinical need? How far should remedying private misfortunes have a claim on communal resources? Do health services have an obligation to enlarge their commitments in line with the expansion of technological feasibility?

The division of opinion among health authorities reflects the fact that these questions are not capable of authoritative resolution. So, for example, the Dutch committee on choices in health care (Dunning 1992) argued that IVF should not be included in any basic package on the grounds that no one has a right to have children, a point further explored in Chapter 9 where we examine the committee's approach to setting priorities. Conversely, the Royal College of Obstetricians and Gynaecologists (1992) has argued that the inability to have children can cause psychological distress and damage – 'the pain of childlessness is every bit as great as that of osteoarthritis of the hip' – and that, consequently, it should be treated like any other medical condition.

The diversity of practice between health authorities in the case of IVF raises a further issue, central to the debate about rationing in the NHS. This is the equity issue. How acceptable is it that IVF should be available in some districts but not in others? If some health authorities provide it, does this set up a presumption that all should do so? If some women can get treatment under the NHS, while others (the majority) have to pay for it in the private sector, does this offend against the equity principle? These questions, while dramatized by the case of IVF, are of course far from unique to it. Another example, at the opposite end of the fertility continuum, is provided by abortion, where health authorities vary greatly in the provision made for carrying out this procedure under the NHS. Both examples simply underline the fact that – as pointed out earlier in this chapter – health authorities vary greatly in the services they make available to their populations. We shall therefore return to this issue when considering, in Chapter 10, whether decisions about priority setting and rationing should be national or local.

THE CASE OF CHILD B

In March 1995 the case of child B – a ten year old girl suffering from leukaemia, subsequently named as Jaymee Bowen – became the most discussed and controversial example of rationing in the history of the NHS. In an action brought by her father, the High Court of Appeal ruled that Cambridge Health Authority had acted rationally and fairly in refusing to spend £75,000 on further treatment for the girl. In doing so, it reversed an earlier High Court judgment. It was a dramatic life-and-death case that lifted the veil on medical decisions about whom to treat, and how, and in doing so provoked an unprecedented national debate about rationing.

The Appeal Court's decision filled the headlines. 'Sentenced to death' ran the lead headline in the *Daily Mail*, and the story underneath began: 'A dying girl's last hope of survival was dramatically crushed yesterday by senior judges.' 'Condemned to her death' was the lead headline in the *Daily Express*, and the story underneath began: 'A girl stricken with leukaemia was last night condemned to die after a court decided she could be refused NHS treatment'. The *Daily Mirror* launched an appeal to pay for the treatment of child B and to fund cancer research. The broadsheets were more restrained in their presentation of the story – though the *Guardian* headline ran 'Dying girl refused NHS treatment' – but nevertheless devoted much space to the story. Commentators were sharply divided. Some supported the decision of the Cambridge Health Authority and the refusal of the Court of Appeal to reverse it (for example, Jenkins 1995b). Others argued that 'Child B must have her treatment, with no conditions attached, no feasibility studies or assessments of financial viability' (Saunders 1995). Media interest produced, in turn, great pressure on the health authority. The health authority's chief executive's house was besieged by reporters; the telephone lines were kept busy, with some 70 per cent of the calls hostile to the authority.

The story behind this explosion of concern about rationing was complex. The account that follows is based on the judgment by the Court of Appeal (Royal Courts of Justice 1995). Jaymee Bowen had been diagnosed as suffering from leukaemia in 1990. Following two rounds of chemotherapy, a bone marrow transplant was carried out in 1994. But in January 1995 she suffered a relapse. The possibility of further treatment – chemotherapy which, if successful, would be followed by a further transplant – was discussed. But the doctor who had been treating her – supported by other specialists – took the view that 'it would not be right to subject B to all this suffering and trauma when the prospects for success were so slight'. This view was supported by a specialist from another hospital – who put the chance of success at 10 per cent – and endorsed by the health authority's director of public health.

In the meantime, however, Jaymee Bowen's father had been taking other medical advice in the United States and elsewhere.

And he had found a doctor – Dr Peter Gravett, who had gone into private practice on retiring from the army – prepared to carry out a second transplant. Dr Gravett took the view that the chance of success (perhaps 20 per cent) was much higher than the various specialists previously consulted had estimated. It was the refusal of Cambridge Health Authority to pay for the proposed treatment by Dr Gravett that prompted the father's appeal to the courts. In the outcome, a private benefactor provided the money needed to pay for treatment. Dr Gravett changed his mind about performing a transplant and, instead, carried out a new therapy: donor lymphocyte infusion (Toynbee 1995). Jaymee Bowen went into remission. In October 1995, when the Court of Appeal lifted an order banning the media from revealing her identity at her father's request so that he could raise funds for further treatment by selling her story, she was quoted as saying: 'I'd rather have gone through more suffering to live than not to go through anything and die'. In the event, Jaymee Bowen died in May 1996.

The story has been told at some length because of the many issues that it raises. In the first place it underlines the difficulty of drawing a boundary between strictly medical considerations about appropriateness and effectiveness, on the one hand, and wider financial considerations about the best use of NHS funds, on the other. The health authority's decision to refuse further funding for the treatment of Jaymee Bowen was based on medical advice, and the views of the specialists involved reflected, in turn, the wider professional consensus as represented by the Children's Cancer Study group. In contrast, Dr Gravett was very much an outsider whose views did not carry any special authority. But the medical advice that the proposed 'aggressive treatment' would be 'detrimental to her quality of life' and that the 'chances of survival were very slight' – to quote the press statement issued after the court judgment – in turn influenced the authority's view that funding would not represent 'an effective use of . . . limited resources'. Medical and financial considerations, in short, were inescapably intertwined. If the medical opinion had been less unanimous, or if the costs involved had not been so large, the decision might well have gone the other way. In this case, moreover, the rules of compassion – the judgement of the doctor treating child B that it was not in Jaymee Bowen's best interest to undergo further treatment – were compatible with, and indeed reinforced, utilitarian considerations. Had there been a conflict, the health authority would have faced a much more agonizing choice.

The case raises further questions. What weight should be given to the *probability* of success in making such resource allocation decisions? Given a cost–utility approach, the answer is not in doubt. In the calculation of the opportunity costs of any given intervention – in a comparison of, for example, treatment for leukaemia and hip replacements – the probability of success is an essential element in the equation. But what if, in a life-at-risk situation such as this, a utilitarian approach is rejected? Does it then make any difference whether the chances of success are 2, 10 or 20 per cent? And if the chances of success have to be weighed not against the opportunity costs but against the pain and suffering involved in undergoing the treatment, who should determine the balance to be struck? Is it the patient, her family or the doctors concerned?

In the case of Jaymee Bowen, her father was – in effect – challenging the right of the medical profession, and of health authorities, to strike such a balance. He was asserting that it was the prerogative of the patient, and only of the patient, to decide whether even an against-the-odds chance of living justified the pains and expenses of treatment. If he had succeeded in his legal challenge to the Cambridge Health Authority, he would therefore have undermined the whole justification of rationing in the NHS, which is that the benefits to individuals have to be offset against the opportunities forgone as a result of treating them. Had his case succeeded, it would have destroyed the foundations of medical paternalism and, with it, the assumption that need (as defined by doctors) must trump demand (as defined by patients).

It was precisely this consideration which persuaded the Court of Appeal to reaffirm the traditional view of judges in the UK, referred to earlier, that it was not for them to interfere in allocative decisions. The judgment of the Master of the Rolls, Sir Thomas Bingham, in effect represented the legal endorsement of utilitarian principles in the allocation of resources in the NHS:

I have no doubt that in a perfect world any treatment which a patient, or a patient's family, sought would be provided if doctors were willing to give it, no matter how much it costs, particularly when a life was potentially at stake. It would, however, in my view, be shutting one's eyes to the real world if the court were to proceed on the basis that we do live in such a world. It is common knowledge that health authorities of all kinds are constantly pressed to make ends meet. They cannot pay their nurses as much as they would like; they cannot provide all the extremely expensive medical equipment that they would like. . . . Difficult and agonising judgments have to be made as to how a limited budget is best allocated to the maximum advantage of the maximum number of patients. That is not a judgment which the court can make.

The case of child B thus had a number of consequences. It strengthened the position of health authorities in taking rationing decisions, giving further legal reinforcement to the view that it was exclusively their responsibility to balance competing claims on limited resources. No wonder the Department of Health, and the NHS Executive, gave their full support to Cambridge Health Authority; had the health authority lost the case, the NHS would have found itself in an extremely embarrassing position of having to meet open-ended demands within a constrained budget. Conversely, however, the case underlined the political costs to health authorities of stripping the veils from medical decision-making. Although Cambridge Health Authority survived the storm, its ordeal by publicity was hardly calculated to encourage others to make explicit decisions – particularly when visible lives are at stake.

THE SUBMERGED ICEBERG

One of the crucial, but usually ignored, aspects of the Jaymee Bowen story is that it only surfaced because the treatment involved an extra contractual referral (ECR). These are referrals that are made to providers not covered by a health authority's normal contracts. In these circumstances, a special case has to be made out to the authority concerned. Thus if the treatment of Jaymee Bowen had involved a provider with whom the health authority had a contract, or indeed if the local doctors treating her had referred her to a tertiary centre, then no special clearance would have been necessary. The treatment would have gone ahead, whatever the expense.

To make this point is a reminder that the screening of ECRs is another and, potentially at least, important form of rationing in the NHS. It is requests for permission to make such referrals which give purchasers an opportunity to limit the availability of services without necessarily making any public declaration about the limits of their menu. There is little systematic knowledge about the extent to which the system of ECRs is used, and how, to screen out demands. It is a low visibility form of rationing. But the available evidence, such as it is, suggests that the criteria used by health authorities when dealing with ECR requests are much the same as those employed when making decisions about what services not to buy: the same, familiar litany of procedures tends to feature in both lists.

However, to raise the issue of ECRs is also to underline just how atypical the case of Jaymee Bowen was. Most decisions about ECRs are far less dramatic in character, though the sums involved may be at least as large. In illustrating this point, we can again draw on the experience of Cambridge Health Authority (Cambridge and Huntingdon Health Commission 1995). The most expensive decisions taken by the authority usually involve not acute care but long-term care. So, for example, the 1995 budget allocated £79,000 for the treatment of a patient in a specialist institution and a similar amount for a patient in a hospital for the mentally ill. Such examples are a reminder that many, perhaps even most, resource allocation decisions in the NHS do not revolve around life and death issues (as in the case of Jaymee Bowen); nor are they necessarily prompted (as in the case of IVF) by expensive technical innovations. They are about the type and level of care that should be provided to people, usually in long-stay institutions, who suffer from chronic conditions that may not be amenable to cure. This is the hidden iceberg of rationing in the NHS.

7

INTO THE SECRET GARDEN

One conclusion emerges strongly from the evidence rehearsed in the previous chapters. This is that, despite all the changes in the structure of the NHS, decisions about which patients should be treated, when and how, remain the prerogative of the health care professions. It is the way in which doctors, nurses and others organize and allocate the resources at their disposal that determines micro rationing at the point of service delivery. This chapter accordingly turns to examining the secret garden of professional practice: the way in which higher level decisions about funding are transmuted into clinical decisions and how resource constraints affect medical judgements about treatment. Unfortunately, the availability of evidence does not match the importance of the subject. There is no shortage of studies of the processes of medical decision-making, from diagnosis to treatment; similarly, there is a plethora of prescriptive models for improving these processes (for a review of the literature, see Dowie and Elstein 1988). But there is remarkably little direct evidence about how funding constraints influence medical decisions or about the criteria used when allocating scarce resources to individual patients.

The paucity of evidence is, in itself, significant. It underlines the extent to which the medical profession's use of its discretion in the allocation of the NHS's resources has hitherto been exempt from scrutiny: the thorny thickets of clinical autonomy surrounding the secret garden have effectively deterred researchers. But it also means that this chapter, rather than being able to give a complete picture, has to rely on fragments of evidence. What follows is therefore the equivalent of trying to reconstruct a dinosaur with only an incomplete set of bones as the starting point for the exercise.

THE DECISION-MAKING CHAIN

The complex and multi-dimensional nature of the resource allocation process in service delivery can best be illustrated by giving a simple, step-by-step account of the decisions involved in translating need as perceived by the patient into action as determined by health care professionals. The process starts from the moment that someone decides to see his or her general practitioner. The GP's receptionist will question and probe before deciding when to give an appointment; in some cases the receptionist's manner may, in itself, be calculated to deter would-be patients, as may the prospect of spending half an hour or so in a gloomy waiting room before actually seeing the doctor. The would-be patient may, at this point, decide not to translate self-defined need into demand for medical attention. If rationing by deterrence fails, rationing by dilution may follow. The GP will decide how much of his or her time to allocate to the particular patient, whether to add to or subtract from the average time of six minutes per consultation, and whether to order any diagnostic tests.

Next comes the decision whether or not to refer the patient to a hospital. If the GP diagnoses a condition like appendicitis or a coronary, an immediate decision to order an ambulance is likely to be taken: here the criterion of resource allocation is, clearly, to give priority to life-threatening conditions. If there is no such urgency, rationing by delay may follow. There will be the wait for an outpatient appointment. Following this, there will be further decisions about what diagnostic tests to order, about whether to make any further outpatient appointments or whether to arrange for a hospital admission. If the decision is to admit the patient to hospital then, again, unless a life-threatening condition is involved, rationing by delay is likely to follow.

Once the patient is admitted to hospital, a further series of resource allocation decisions follow. What, and how many, diagnostic tests should be carried out? What treatment should be given? Once treated, the question of rationing by termination arises: how quickly should the patient be discharged? These are all medical decisions. But to concentrate exclusively on them is to give a one-dimensional picture of rationing in the NHS: it is to conflate health care with medical care. The way in which the patient experiences hospital treatment will also be affected by a variety of other, non-medical decisions about the allocation of resources. There will be decisions about how many nursing and other staff to allocate to a particular ward, about the time physiotherapists should devote to individual patients, about how much to spend on food for patients.

The importance of such non-medical decisions about priorities in the allocation of resources at the point of service delivery must be stressed all the more since they rarely feature in debates about rationing, though they may greatly affect the quality of care offered to patients. These decisions tend to lack visibility; they offer great scope for gradual dilution over time. They are most important, in terms of their impact, in precisely those sectors of health care which constitute what we called in Chapter 6 the hidden iceberg of rationing, i.e. those that are least open to public scrutiny, where the patients concerned may be seen as deviant and where the role of the medical profession is often marginal. Only occasionally and sporadically, when there is a scandal or when public concern is aroused, do the effects of resource allocation policies become apparent.

WHAT FACTORS INFLUENCE DECISIONS?

One of the best documented phenomena in the NHS is the variation between general practitioners in the number of patients they refer to hospitals (Farrow and Jewell 1993). Rates of referral range from 2.5 to 5.4 per 100 consultations and from 4.0 to 13.2 per 100 patients on the general practitioner's list. And the available evidence so far suggests that GP fundholding has as yet done little to change referral patterns (Surender *et al.* 1995). Access to specialist hospital care, it seems, is largely a function of how individual GPs interpret their gatekeeping role. A variety of factors influence their decisions. The availability of local services is certainly one of them; if there are long waiting lists or no facilities, they may not refer patients. GPs may, in other words, incorporate hospital rationing practices into their own referral policies, a point to which we return below when considering decision-making in the case of treatment for end stage renal disease. However, this does not seem to be the only, or even the main, reason for variations in referral rates. GPs vary in the way they see their professional role and how they rate their own skills; similarly, they vary in how they assess the competence and style of specialists; lastly, they vary in the weight they give to the wishes, or persistence, of patients. In other words, the rationing of access to specialist services by GP tends to be a highly idiosyncratic process, affected but not determined by the availability of resources.

Moving to the specialist sector, idiosyncratic variation between consultants is again the norm, not only in the way they practise but also in the way they manage access to services. The relationship between the lengths of waiting lists and times and the availability of resources remains unresolved (Harvey 1993). The criteria used by consultants in managing the queuing system, in deciding priorities between patients on waiting lists, remain obscure. Most hospitals operate a three-point scale of urgency: immediate, urgent and non-urgent (West 1993). But it is far from clear how these criteria are applied in practice: how far there is agreement between consultants in the way they define 'urgency' and whether the concept is stable over time or changes with the availability of resources. It is precisely because of this opaqueness that waiting lists, as Frankel and West (1993) have argued, 'permit a blurring of the National Health Service's capacity for or commitment to certain sorts of treatment. Waiting lists veil the discrepancies between what is offered and what can be done.'

One of the very few studies of the way in which consultants prioritize between patients (Lack and Fletcher 1993) does, however, lift a small corner of the veil. This examined the factors taken into account by consultants at one hospital in determining priority for surgery for patients on their waiting lists. By far the most important factor, it turned out, was the progression of the disease, i.e. the consultant's judgement that the patient's condition would deteriorate in the absence of intervention. The degree of pain and disability and the effect of the condition on the patient's capacity to function also influenced decisions, but to a much lesser extent. However, it cannot be assumed that this study necessarily provides a representative view. Further, the evidence suggests that the kind of criteria used – and the weight given to them – in deciding priorities for patients on waiting lists for elective surgery are not necessarily used universally. Other criteria appear to be used when it comes to life-threatening conditions.

Chief among these, it seems, is age (Grimley Evans 1993). The case of treatment for end stage renal failures illustrates the point, as already noted in Chapter 4. Age is not the only criterion for the selection of patients for treatment: in the case of dialysis, in particular, decisions about whether or not to treat also revolve around judgements about the patient's psychological and social capacity to sustain the strains involved (Halper 1989). But age does seem to be the factor most often invoked to deny treatment. It provides an automatic pilot for doctors, so simplifying the perplexities, and avoiding the agonies, of choosing between different lives.

The justification for using the age of the patient as a cut-off point for offering treatment is less than clear. For age could be used as a criterion for denying treatment for a number of rather different reasons. It could be used because of the 'fair innings' argument, i.e. that scarce resources should be used for the benefit of those who have their lives still ahead of them, rather than for those who have already had a chance to develop their full potentials. A related, utilitarian-type argument would be that the treatment of younger candidates for treatment would yield more 'life years', i.e. that the cost per year gained as a result of intervention – whether or not adjusted to take account of its quality – is lower in the case of young patients. Alternatively, age may be used as a proxy for the capacity to benefit from treatment: the elderly may not have as good a prognosis as the young. This, however, is an argument which is more convincing when applied to the elderly as a group rather than to them individually. Indeed, it could lead to an elderly person with a good prognosis being denied treatment while a young person with a poor prognosis is offered it – a warning against using information about groups as a decision rule for allocating resources to individuals within them.

The treatment of renal dialysis also offers a warning about another principle much invoked in justifying resource allocation decisions: that of appropriateness. This is an individual rather than group orientated criterion. It assumes that the doctors concerned can make a judgement both about the patient's need for treatment and about his or her capacity to benefit from it. The trouble is that doctors differ in the judgements they make. The point is well illustrated by a study which involved sending 16 case histories of a variety of patients with end stage renal failure to a large number of general practitioners, consultants and specialist nephrologists (Challah *et al.* 1984), and asking them what treatment, if any, was appropriate. GPs and non-specialist consultants, it turned out, rejected more cases for treatment than nephrologists. In turn, as another study (Parsons and Lock 1980) found, nephrologists do not always agree. When nephrologists were presented with data about 20 patients, no one patient was rejected by everyone. If age is an over-rigid criterion for the denial of treatment, inasmuch as it is

insensitive to the characteristics of individual patients, appropriateness would seem to be an over-elastic one, inasmuch as it gives
play to idiosyncratic interpretations by individual clinicians.

The case of treatment for end stage renal failure has been
examined at some length because it is unusually well documented
and because it provides an opportunity to explore a variety of
issues. But it is far from unique. Consider, for example, acute care
for cases of myocardial infarction. The professional consensus, as
expressed by the Royal College of Physicians, is that there are no
clinical reasons for restricting cardiological interventions on the
ground of age alone. Yet a fifth of coronary care units have an upper
age limit for admissions and two-fifths have an upper age limit for
thrombolytic therapy (Elder and Fox 1992). This leads to what has
been called the 'rationing paradox' (Pollock 1995). While the risk of
death following intervention in a 70 year old with a myocardial
infarction is four times that of someone below 60, the greatest
benefits from treatment (in terms of lives saved) will accrue in the
older age group, simply because this is where the incidence of
coronary heart disease is highest.

Other factors, apart from age, also influence the selection of
patients for treatment. Most controversially, some consultants
refuse coronary by-pass surgery or transplants to patients who
refuse to give up smoking. Here the argument, as put in an article in
the *British Medical Journal*, is that 'Patients who smoke spend
longer in hospital and have poorer results. Treating them deprives
patients who have never smoked or who have stopped smoking of
more efficient and effective surgery' (Underwood and Bailey 1993).
In other words, denial of treatment seemed to be based on the
capacity to benefit principle, although lurking in the background
there also appears to be an appeal to the notion of desert: smokers
are seen as less deserving since their bad habit may have contributed
to the condition for which they are seeking treatment.

The article provoked much controversy and many responses in
the letter columns of the *British Medical Journal*. It was illogical to
pick out smoking, it was argued, when drinking or over-working
might well have the same effect on the patient's prospects of
survival. Above all, the correspondence brought out into the open
the clash between the ethical individualists and the utilitarians in the
medical profession. On the one hand, the rule of rescue was much
invoked: medical ethics demanded that life saving surgery should be
carried out despite the risks of post-operative complications.
Further, it was unethical, one correspondent asserted, to deny a

patient the benefit of any treatment simply to reduce failure rates. On the other hand, it was argued that treating smokers represented a waste of the NHS's resources, since they consumed more resources than non-smokers with worse results.

The controversy about the denial of treatment to smokers also provides a hint – no more – about another implicit criterion of selection: creaming. Doctors may prefer to treat amenable or interesting patients and may select out those whom they consider to be troublesome or unrewarding. In the words of one correspondent (Mamode 1993), 'The doctor carries a latent resentment of the patient who represents more work and stress, and this occasionally surfaces when the opportunity to castigate the patient arises, particularly if the patient's behaviour threatens to undo hours of hard work'. The evidence on this point is elusive and largely anecdotal. However, our interviews with purchasers suggest that this kind of selection is not limited either to the acute sector or to the medical profession but may be a more pervasive phenomenon in the NHS. Purchasers report examples of providers selecting out people they did not want to deal with: mental health workers avoiding contact, if possible, with severely mentally ill people and speech therapists preferring middle-class children as clients to more difficult cases. In other words, they allocate resources according to the responsiveness or acceptability of the client, a strategy designed, unconsciously no doubt, to make life more interesting or less stressful for themselves. In this respect, they are no different from professionals or bureaucrats in other services (Lipsky 1980) – like academics who prefer to devote their time to bright graduate students rather than engaging in the slog of trying to arouse the interest of first-year undergraduates.

ARE BRITISH DOCTORS DIFFERENT?

So far the focus of this analysis has been on how doctors in the NHS set about rationing. The main theme that has emerged has been the extent of the variations within the medical profession, in terms both of practice and of the views held about the principles that should shape rationing policies. If, however, we substitute the telescope for the microscope – if, instead of examining British practice in detail, we ask whether there are some characteristics that distinguish practice in the NHS from other health care systems – does a different picture emerge? In other words, do the variations conceal

Learning Resources

a systemic bias? To answer these questions, we examine in this section the findings of the first, and still much quoted, general study of rationing in the NHS, that by Aaron and Schwartz (1984).

The main findings of this study were that, compared to the United States, the NHS 'clearly rationed' many services. The overall rate for a variety of procedures, ranging from hip replacements to chemotherapy for cancer, was much higher in the USA than in the UK. Similarly, the overall use of various diagnostic technological tools, ranging from computerized tomography scanners to diagnostic X-rays, was much higher in the USA than in the UK. In short, there is indeed a systemic bias towards under-treatment. British doctors, Aaron and Schwartz argue, 'seek medical justification for decisions forced on them by resource limits. Doctors gradually redefine standards of care so that they can escape the constant recognition that financial limits compel them to do less than their best.'

There are, however, problems in drawing any conclusions from this study. They stem from the fact that the level of provision in the United States is taken as the benchmark of adequacy for the NHS. The assumption is that if a given procedure is carried out less frequently in Britain, if a given diagnostic technique is used less frequently, then this is in itself evidence of rationing. This is highly questionable. It could rather more plausibly be argued that the US levels of activity represent the pathology of a system where the incentives are to maximize activity rather than effectiveness. This has been precisely the conclusion drawn in the USA: witness the continuing debate about how to reform American health care so as to eliminate perverse incentives (Marmor 1994).

The argument that British doctors internalize resource constraints, and adapt their style of clinical practice accordingly, is more plausible. Indeed, it is in line with the evidence rehearsed in this and previous chapters. But even here there is a need for caution. As a former President of the Royal College of Physicians has argued (Hoffenberg 1987), Aaron and Schwartz fail to consider the possibility that British doctors 'might actually be more discerning' and 'less inclined to squeeze the last drop of potential benefit from any form of treatment'. And he cited the following example – long before the case of child B – to illustrate the differences in American and British attitudes:

My awareness of this difference in approach was heightened during a recent visit to America where I attended a meeting to discuss the ethics of withholding treatment from a young infant with a rare form of congenital leukaemia. The infant had been given a course of treatment no different from those that had already been reported to be unsuccessful in similar cases. The side effects had been severe – vomiting, diarrhoea, anaemia, and bleeding from platelet inhibitions; a very short and incomplete remission had been achieved. The question was whether a second course of chemotherapy was justified. After discussion with the parents and a debate by doctors, nurses, social workers, psychologists, a professor of medical ethics and, of course, the hospital lawyer, the decision was taken not to go ahead. In Britain, I suspect, the approach would have been different. The first course of chemotherapy would not have been given, and this decision would have been taken by the doctors, the parents being informed that the only known treatment was both ineffective and likely to cause undesirably severe side-effects. I have no doubt that our own approach would have been more humane.

Much the same point could be made about the American bias towards heroic (and very expensive) efforts to prolong the life of even the very old, even if only for a few months (Callahan 1990). In other words, definitions and perceptions of rationing may depend on the cultural context and the way institutions determine expectations. In a society like the United States, which believes in the perfectibility of mankind and where health care is demand driven, anything short of what is technically possible will be seen as rationing. In an original sin society like Britain, where decay and death are seen as part of the human condition and where medical paternalism defines the limits of health care, delivering less than the optimum will be seen not as rationing but as a humane exercise of clinical judgement.

But clinical judgment is fallible. The American and British systems offer, as already argued, very different incentives to clinicians. In the former, the incentives are to maximize activity; in the latter, they are to maximize effectiveness. This, indeed, is the justification for the kind of selection policies – including the denial of treatment – reviewed in this chapter. It might therefore be expected that British clinicians would be less prone to make inappropriate decisions than their American counterparts. However, the evidence on this point is at best ambiguous. Lower rates of intervention do not necessarily mean that they are better targeted.

In a study which tested the decisions of both British and American clinicians to carry out coronary angiography and coronary by-pass surgery against agreed criteria of appropriateness, no great differences appeared between the two groups: in both cases a 'substantial' proportion of the procedures were carried out inappropriately (Bernstein *et al.* 1993).

One conclusion that could be drawn from this is that the criteria used may have been too mechanistic and that they may have made inadequate allowance for the characteristics of the individual patients involved. But another conclusion could be that no account of clinical decision-making about the allocation of resources is complete without taking into account the role of uncertainty in medicine: a conclusion which, in turn, helps to explain one of the main themes of this chapter, the variability and idiosyncracy of so much practice in the way resources are allocated.

MEDICINE AND UNCERTAINTY

The management of scarce resources by doctors involves also the management of uncertainty (Mechanic 1979, 1992). This has two related dimensions. First, there is ignorance about what does or does not work. Thus it has been estimated that only 15 per cent of medical interventions are supported by solid scientific evidence (Smith 1991a). And even when there is such evidence, it is not cast in concrete for all times: 'Today's medical facts may often be no more than current hypotheses, liable to be disproved and modified by new evidence' (McPherson 1994). Second, even assuming that there is solid evidence, there remains the problem of applying it to the specific circumstances of an individual patient.

Uncertainty begins with the process of making a diagnosis. As the editor of the *New England Journal of Medicine* (cited in Mechanic 1992: 1721) put it:

> In many ways the diagnostic process resembles the start of a chess game. After one or two moves (one or two symptoms) the number of possible moves (diagnostic possibilities) is usually enormous; in both chess and medicine, the object is to win, but the challenge is to make the right move in the right direction at the right time. Unfortunately, the route is never clear in advance.

Uncertainty is further compounded when it comes to deciding on treatment following a diagnosis. There is usually a multiple choice.

The decision taken will depend on a variety of factors. For, as a distinguished American physician has pointed out (Eddy 1988), the 'value of any particular procedure depends on who performs it, on whom it is performed and the circumstances of performance'. In particular, the characteristics of the patients concerned will affect the choice made. To quote a study of medical decision-making (K. M. Hunter 1991):

> Even if the physical phenomena remain the same from one patient to another with the same disease, the perception and interpretation of what is regarded as 'fact' as well as the ramifying circumstances affecting the patient will be subtly, sometimes markedly, different. The decision to offer only medical treatment to one man with angina, for example, while another will be led towards coronary artery bypass surgery may have to do with the patient's response to therapy, his reliability as a manager of his own medication, or his attitude towards risk. These circumstances can be understood and reliably assessed only as part of the physician's ongoing understanding of the patient.

Lastly, there is uncertainty about the likely outcome of any treatment once the choice has been made. Prediction is difficult. To quote Eddy again, 'The central problem is that there is a natural variation in the way people respond to a medical procedure. Take two people who, to the best of our ability to define such things, are identical in all important respects, submit them to the same operative procedure, and one will die on the operating table while the other will not.'

The role of uncertainty is, however, not only critical for understanding why there is so much variation in the way doctors practise – both between health care systems and within them – and why there is so much scope for medical discretion in the allocation of resources and the criteria used in making decisions. It is also central when analysing alternative strategies for setting priorities and rationing: the topic addressed in the concluding chapters, where we turn to examining the different solutions on offer. Accepting that the 'dominant medical paradigm of scientific truth and certainty' (McPherson 1994) is to a large extent a fiction, or at best an exaggeration, has profound implications for the way in which we think about the management of scarce resources. The theme of 'uncertainty' will therefore provide a thread running through what follows.

PART III

THE WAY AHEAD

8

MONEY OR SCIENCE
TO THE RESCUE?

The assumption shaping the analysis so far has been that priority setting and rationing are inevitable in the NHS, as in any system of service delivery operating within budget constraints. From this perspective, the only relevant issues are who should take the decisions about allocating scarce resources, how they should be made and what criteria should be used. But is this assumption correct? This chapter addresses this question directly. It does so by examining the two very different types of argument that are usually invoked to deny the inevitability of rationing. The first is that the phenomenon of rationing in the NHS – in its many dimensions – simply reflects the fact that it is underfunded. In other words, government parsimony is to blame. The second is that there would be no need for rationing if only the knowledge generated by science were fully utilized. In other words, ignorance is to blame. The logic of the two arguments is very different. The case for a more generous budget rests on the presumption that available resources are fully stretched and that the gap between supply and demand can therefore only be bridged by making more funds available. The appeal to science rests on the presumption that resources are at present being wasted because they are not used efficiently or effectively and that scarcity is therefore largely (if not wholly) self-induced. However, it could just be that a *combination* of extra funds and the elimination of waste would resolve the dilemmas of choice in the allocation of resources. Accordingly, in what follows we test the plausibility of each argument in turn.

THE CASE FOR EXTRA FUNDING

The NHS, as we saw in Chapter 4, institutionalizes scarcity. Its budget is determined neither by demand nor by need, both of which are in any case elusive and elastic concepts and neither of which is independent of supply. It is the product of history, modified by political and economic considerations. If health care professionals succeed in convincing the public that the NHS is on the point of collapse because of inadequate funding – as they have attempted to do roughly every three years throughout the NHS's existence – governments are apt to turn generous, particularly when a general election is looming. If the British economy does well, so usually does the NHS; if the British economy coughs, the NHS tends to catch cold.

The NHS budget is therefore a peculiar construct. It is the product of a series of decisions, reflecting political expediency, and economic luck, taken over the five decades of its existence. There is no formula – as a succession of Committees of Inquiry and Royal Commissions have agreed – which allows governments or their critics to determine the 'right' or 'appropriate' level of funding. There have, indeed, been attempts to devise a method for calculating the annual increment in the NHS budget by extrapolating past patterns of activity and expenditure and adjusting them for changes in demography and technology. There is a problem about this: why assume that past patterns are necessarily a good guide to the future? Even leaving this objection aside, however, there is a still more fundamental difficulty with this type of approach: it begs the crucial question of the adequacy (or otherwise) of the base line budget (Klein 1995). There is little point, after all, in getting the increments right if the starting point is wrong. And certainly it will not help us to determine a level of funding which will make rationing unnecessary. Extrapolating from the past means, in the case of the NHS, also perpetuating rationing.

Nor does an appeal to the experience of other countries help. There is no difficulty in demonstrating that other countries spend a great deal more on health care than Britain. In the early 1990s, expenditure on health care as a proportion of the gross domestic product ranged from 7.1 per cent in the United Kingdom to 14 per cent in the USA. In the advanced, post-industrial countries, France (9.4), Germany (8.7), the Netherlands (8.6) and Sweden (7.9) were in the middle of the range, while Denmark (6.5) and Japan (6.9) were at the bottom (OECD 1994). Indeed, the contrast between

Britain and other countries can be made more dramatic still by translating the percentage of the national income spent into expenditure per head of population, thus underlining the parsimony of the NHS.

But this does not prove that the NHS is 'underfunded'. Higher expenditure in other countries may mean that health care staff are more highly paid or that resources are used less efficiently. Far less do international comparisons permit the conclusion that spending more would eliminate the need for priority setting or rationing. Indeed, invoking international comparisons to justify spending more on the NHS and using comparative data to argue that rationing is not inevitable is to confuse two conceptually very distinct arguments. There may well be a case for arguing, quite irrespective of what other countries do, that more should be spent on the NHS – that the physical condition of many NHS hospitals is a disgrace, that staffing levels in some areas are dangerously low, that the policy of care in the community has become a synonym for inadequacy and so on – a case that could have been made throughout the history of the NHS. But to list the competing claims for extra resources is also to underline that choices between them would still have to be made even if the Chancellor of the Exchequer were to have a reckless fit of pre-election generosity. The paradox is that the longer the catalogue of the NHS's inadequacies – on which the case for underfunding rests – the greater, seemingly, is the inevitability of prioritizing and rationing.

International comparisons reinforce, if anything, this conclusion. The fact that the United States spends twice as much of its national income on health care as Britain has not eliminated rationing there. As already noted, the literature on rationing speaks with a strong American accent. There is rationing by exclusion, i.e. the 30 million or so people who are uninsured and therefore have to rely on access via the emergency room. There is rationing by denial: insurance policies routinely include clauses which limit the scope of the coverage offered. There is rationing by dilution: of the 2000 community care centres that were to have been built by 1980 to accommodate those decanted from mental hospitals, only 600 have been provided (Moynihan 1996).

The US example can, of course, be dismissed as one more instance of the peculiar perversities – famine among plenty – produced by the system there. But it is difficult to sustain that view of American exceptionalism if we turn to those countries which take the rationing issue seriously enough to appoint special commissions to consider it. These include, as we shall see in the next chapter, the Netherlands, Sweden, Canada, New Zealand and Norway. Not only do all of these spend more on health care than Britain, they also differ in the way health care is organized. The fact of rationing therefore seems to be independent both of the level of funding and of the structure of any specific health care system, though the form that it takes, the way it is perceived and the degree of visibility that it has may well vary from country to country.

The one common element in all these countries, the United States apart, is that the level of health care spending is determined by collective decisions. As in the case of the NHS, therefore, the claims of the health care system for funding have to be weighed against the competing claims of other services or programmes (some of which may have at least as much impact on the population's health status as expenditure on medical services). In turn, the different claims of the component parts of the health care system have to be weighed against each other. Hence the Swedish Parliamentary Priorities Commission (1995) concluded that: 'Prioritisation due to resource constraints has always existed and will always be necessary in the caring sector'. If the issue has risen to the top of the international agenda of debate about health care it is because those 'resource constraints' have become more severe under the twin pressures of governments seeking to restrain the growth of public expenditure and rising demand for health care as the result of demographic and other trends.

But if rationing characterizes the collective provision of health care, irrespective of the level of expenditure, one possible conclusion is that this demonstrates a fundamental flaw in such systems. This has been precisely the conclusion drawn in the case of the NHS. Rationing, it has been argued, is the inevitable product of a system where the individual will demand more services as a consumer than he or she is prepared to finance as a taxpayer (Buchanan 1965). Given predominantly free services, there are no incentives to restrain demand, while everyone has an incentive to keep down taxes. From this flows the argument that supply and demand would come into balance – so eliminating the need for rationing – if only collective provision were replaced by insurance schemes and charges for services. Instead of the level of funding for health care being determined by political decisions it would be driven by individual preferences. As a result, more money would flow into the system.

Whatever else may be said in favour of such a system of health care provision, it cannot plausibly be argued that it would eliminate the need for rationing as distinct from changing its form. It would introduce rationing by price. And since governments would have to pay the insurance premiums of those who cannot afford to do so for themselves, there would still have to be a political decision as to the appropriate level of funding. If, for example, health care insurance were to be based on a system of vouchers (Harris and Seldon 1979), a way would have to be found of fixing their value. The basic package of health care to be assured to everyone would therefore have to be defined. This is, of course, precisely why the Dutch government set up its committee on choices in health care in an attempt to define the basic entitlements that should be covered by all insurance schemes. Expelled from the front door, rationing creeps in by the back door.

This conclusion is reinforced if we unpackage the notion of health care. The demand for acute *medical* care of the type that features in most debates about rationing – i.e. the use of medical technology to prolong life or to improve human functioning – could conceivably prove to be finite, contrary to conventional wisdom. Medical treatment has costs, such as pain and anxiety, even if there is no price; further, a point comes when there are no more joints or organs left to replace. However, it is more difficult to set limits to the level of *health* care that should be provided to support those who suffer from chronic or disabling conditions and to make their lives more tolerable. This is perhaps the greatest challenge to health care systems (Fox 1993), accentuated by the ageing of the populations being served. But it also represents a peculiarly open-ended commitment, since definitions of adequacy are likely to shift over time. For example, if it is desirable that residents in nursing homes should have their own rooms, it is surely just as desirable that they should have their own bathrooms, and so on. Here it seems realistic to assume that the definition of acceptability will move upward in line with rising living standards and expectations. The social imperative may be as powerful a driving force as the technological imperative.

There is yet a further consideration which should dampen optimism about the feasibility of satisfying all extra claims for resources as the result of a fit of generosity by Chancellors of the Exchequer or through changing the system of finance. This is that the cost of providing any given level of health care tends to rise over time, i.e. even standing still becomes ever more expensive (Baumol 1995). Health care is a labour, rather than a capital, intensive industry: something like 70 per cent of the NHS's budget is spent on pay. It is therefore also an industry where productivity tends to rise more slowly than in the rest of the economy: investment in new health care technology may extend the limits of the possible, or improve quality, but only rarely contributes to an increase in output or a decrease in costs. But the level of salaries and wages tends to rise in line with the productivity-driven increases in the rest of the economy: hence the persistent rise in the cost of delivering any given bundle of services. The rate of such 'cost inflation' varies between systems. Those systems which are virtual monopoly employers of doctors and nurses – like Britain's or Sweden's – are conspicuously more successful in containing cost inflation than the United States. However, the long-term trend everywhere is the same. Spending more, insofar as it may simply mean paying everyone working in health care more, does not necessarily translate into improved services.

Neither greater generosity in the financing of collective health care systems, nor their replacement by systems driven by individual preferences, can provide a way of escaping the dilemmas of choice. Even if more funds were to be made available for health care in Britain, decisions between competing claims on resources would still have to be taken. Accordingly, the next section examines whether science can provide an answer.

WHAT SCIENCE OFFERS

The appeal to science starts from the assumption that scarcity is largely – if not wholly – a self-induced phenomenon. It is perceived to be the result of a failure both to mobilize science to generate knowledge about what does or does not work and to use existing evidence to change practice. Scarcity, in short, is a function of ignorance and mismanagement: of a failure to harness knowledge and to ensure the best use of available resources (see, for example, Roberts 1995). If health care systems could only eliminate waste, if only inefficient or ineffective services and procedures could be eliminated, then the resources so freed would allow all the frustrated demands to be satisfied. There would be no more waiting lists. There would be no more need to make agonized decisions about priorities between services. There would be no more need to ration by denial or dilution.

The concept of 'waste' turns out, on closer inspection, to be a chameleon concept. In the 1980s and early 1990s the assumption was that the NHS would eradicate waste and improve efficiency by introducing better management. And there was much reason for thinking that the lengths of waiting lists, for example, reflected as much poor organization as inadequate resources. By the mid-1990s, however, the consequent rise in spending on management was, in itself, seen by many as an example of waste. And the emphasis increasingly switched to increasing efficiency and effectiveness by invoking the new scientism (Klein 1996). Scientific knowledge would be applied to solving the NHS's problems. The NHS Executive, as noted in Chapter 5, exhorted health authorities to purchase only procedures with demonstrable beneficial outcomes. Clinical practice was to be based on the systematic, scientific evaluation of the effectiveness of health care interventions.

The NHS invested considerable resources, as well as faith, in the new orthodoxy (NHS Executive 1996). A comprehensive research programme, designed to generate the knowledge base for evidence based medicine, was launched. Academic centres were set up to synthesize the available evidence and to diffuse the results. The Royal Colleges produced a series of guidelines designed to set out the consensus about best practice in the treatment of specific conditions. And national activity was mirrored at the local level, as we saw in Chapter 6, where health authorities encouraged the production of guidelines and protocols (although the latter term is disliked by many clinicians as implying an unacceptable degree of specificity in defining what should be done).

The case for the new scientism is, at first sight, overwhelmingly persuasive. If there is no evidence for the effectiveness of most forms of medical intervention (see Chapter 7), then it seems reasonable to assume that a great deal of money is being wasted on procedures and treatments that are not doing patients any good: a conclusion reinforced by the fact that there *is* evidence that many clinicians persevere with procedures and forms of treatment long after they have been demonstrated to be ineffective or inappropriate. Similarly, if there are large variations between doctors in the way they use resources, with little evidence that high rates of activity or use of resources lead to better health outcomes for patients, it again seems reasonable to assume that a great deal of money could be saved by bringing practice into line with what the more parsimonious clinicians are already doing.

The logic of this line of argument might even suggest that expenditure on the NHS, far from needing to be raised in order to accommodate the competing claims for extra resources, could be cut. For if demonstrable effectiveness, based on scientific evidence, is to be the only criterion for purchasing, if the onus of proof is to be on doctors to show that their interventions improve outcomes, then most of the existing services provided by the NHS would fail the test and could be scrapped. No wonder ministers and managers embraced the new faith with enthusiasm. For it appeared to offer them the prospect of less pain, less responsibility for taking difficult decisions and a legitimate way of curbing what were often perceived to be the idiosyncratic and extravagant practices of doctors.

Before leaping to this conclusion, however, it is important to recognize the limits, as well as the potentials, of the new scientism. We have already had occasion to question the robustness of some of the central concepts, such as 'effectiveness' and 'appropriateness', in the rhetoric of the new scientism when examining the attempts of health authorities to apply them in practice. Here we bring together the various strands of our analysis to argue that the hopes invested in developing knowledge based medicine and evidence based purchasing – and instruments like guidelines – may be exaggerated. The new scientism offers great scope for improving the quality of medicine and health care but is not a philosopher's stone for converting scarcity into plenty.

In the first place, the new scientism is not the only source of authoritative knowledge. There is also the experiential knowledge of the medical profession. The point is well caught in the following quotation from the President of the Royal College of Surgeons, Sir Norman Browse, giving evidence to the House of Commons Health Committee (1995):

> There has never been a clinical trial on removing or not removing an acutely-inflamed appendix. You know of the complications which occur if you do not remove it; you know that it is the right thing to do. Just because there have not been double-blind, randomly allocated clinical trials of everything, that does not mean to say that the knowledge which has been accumulated since the Dark Ages finished in about 1415 does not mean anything. You must not go away with this notion that we are all being ineffective, we do not know what we are doing or, for that matter, that we do not *look* at what we are doing and change if we find something is ineffective.

Next, consider the notion of effectiveness, which tends to be used as though it were self-evidently unproblematic. This, on closer examination, turns out to be a slippery concept (Blustein and Marmor

1992). The effectiveness of a medical intervention is a function of its outcome: hence, of course, the current emphasis on research to increase knowledge about outcomes. But rolling back the frontiers of ignorance, however desirable in itself, may turn out to be a Sisyphean task. Even randomized controlled trials (RCTs), which are often seen as the gold standard for evaluating medical innovations, may not be appropriate in all circumstances. Innovation is often a stepwise process, involving the modification of existing procedures over time, and it is not clear at what stage in the process evaluation should take place (Jennett 1986). Outcomes may, furthermore, be contingent on their setting: the question may often be not how a given procedure works in its place of origin but how it would fare in different environments when applied on a mass production scale by practitioners who may be less skilled in the techniques concerned; the use of keyhole surgery provides a case in point. Lastly, the notion of outcomes is itself contestable (Carr-Hill 1995). Over what time should outcomes be measured? And whose valuation of outcomes – those of the health care professionals or of patients – should be used? Moreover, the results of scientific trials may not be easy to interpret: at least one study (Fahey *et al.* 1995) has shown how the way in which the evidence is presented may influence the conclusions drawn.

Assuming that such problems can be overcome – that science can indeed conquer ignorance – some forms of intervention will undoubtedly turn out to be demonstrably ineffective, in which case, of course, the waste involved in their use can be eliminated to the benefit of all (including the patients subjected to the treatment). Some mass screening programmes fall into this category (Russell 1994) The history of medicine, it has been pointed out (McKee and Clarke 1995), is full of treatments that were once popular but are now known to be valueless. But more often the evidence may well be more ambiguous and suggest that a given intervention is only selectively effective: that its effects are uncertain and contingent on the circumstances of individual patients. This is so, for example, even in the case of glue ear discussed in Chapter 6. Here the evidence suggested that the indiscriminate insertion of grommets was wasteful. The fact that inserting grommets may often be unnecessary does not demonstrate, however, that this is always so. Evidence about heterogeneous groups, to reiterate, does not necessarily help to make decisions about individuals.

In the case of life-threatening conditions, moreover, patients may be willing to risk enduring treatment even though evidence of effectiveness may be lacking and the chances of success are extremely slim. They may feel, as in the case of child B and of AIDS patients demanding drugs whose efficacy had not yet been demonstrated, that there is nothing to lose by gambling. As Blustein and Marmor (1992) argue, 'It is implausible to expect that heart-disease victims would quietly forgo potentially lifesaving treatment in the name of scientific purity'.

More troubling still, there are treatments which are demonstrably effective but where questions may be raised about the appropriateness of investing resources in them. To demonstrate that buttock lift or breast augmentation (to cite some of the procedures that are excluded by many health authorities from their shopping lists) succeed in re-engineering the anatomy and reinvigorating the patient's psyche does not dispose of argument about whether such treatment should be offered by the NHS. Similarly, to demonstrate that IVF (to return to one of the issues that divides health authorities when deciding what to buy) does result in the production of babies does not automatically set up a presumption that it should be provided by the NHS. 'These controversies', to quote Blustein and Marmor again, 'often reflect fundamental disagreements about the goals and obligations of providers, payers and patients, or even disputes about the significance of human lives'. And as economists are quick to point out, evidence about effectiveness does not tell us anything about allocative efficiency. If the opportunity costs of investing in any given procedure are taken into account, an effective intervention may still be deemed to represent a misuse of resources because of its high price.

There are further difficulties when evidence about effectiveness, and good practice, is translated into guidelines for clinical practice. These have been set out by Hopkins (1995), who heads the Research Unit of the Royal College of Physicians and has himself been deeply involved in their production. Guidelines tend to deal with medical diagnoses, not medical problems. They tend to deal with specific disorders, although a high proportion of the patients admitted to hospital have multiple problems. Above all, the kind of evidence needed to design guidelines is usually lacking when it comes to dealing with 'chronic disorders and the results of ageing, for which the technical interventions that are available do not influence outcome very much'. Nor are clinical guidelines suitable for the management of those cases where 'patients and their families have to modify their lives to accommodate the illness, rather than expect technical relief'. In short, guidelines may be most problematic in precisely those areas of health care whose importance – in terms of the number of lives affected – is in an inverse relationship to their public visibility, lacking as they do the high profile of dramatic technological interventions.

To make these points is not to dismiss the utility of guidelines. By promoting medical self-education and self-examination – by diffusing knowledge about state of the art of medicine – guidelines can help to enhance the quality of health care. It is, however, to question the scope for, and desirability of, using guidelines as instruments for cutting costs by controlling medical practice. This appears to be the long-term hope of the NHS Executive, which 'commends' certain guidelines to purchasers in the hope that they will be incorporated into the contracting process. But if guidelines are to control practice, they have to be specific in their criteria for every step in the diagnostic process and treatment of patients if compliance is to be monitored. In turn, monitoring compliance would require extra information to be generated. Overall, therefore, the cost of attempting to eliminate 'waste' may be heavy in terms of extra bureaucracy and may additionally, as American experience suggests (Mechanic 1995), generate conflict and frustration by infringing on professional autonomy.

The expectation that guidelines and protocols can be used to promote 'best buy' purchasing seems to rest on an over-simple model of the professional decision making process by taking the claim of medicine to be considered a science at face value. As McKee and Clarke (1995) have argued, the proponents of guideline based purchasing 'may have paid insufficient attention to the uncertainty inherent in clinical practice, with the imposition of a spurious rationality on a sometimes inherently irrational process'.

Overall, therefore, it does not seem plausible to assume that the mobilization of science will necessarily – or even probably – dispose of the necessity for making painful choices in the allocation of resources. Evidence about effectiveness may inform those choices, just as it may improve the quality of what is offered. Similarly, guidelines may be a way of promoting good practice and giving visibility to the criteria used by the medical profession when rationing resources. But, as in the case of the argument that greater generosity in the funding of the NHS would obviate the need for choice, so the assumption that science can do the trick turns out to rest on a delusion. To quote the Director of Public Health of the Cambridge Health Commission (Zimmern 1995),

even if purchasers were able to remove at a stroke all procedures agreed to be inefficient and ineffective, the resources
released would almost immediately be consumed by the tide of
unmet need for the remaining efficient and effective interventions. Thresholds for referral would drop and patients,
previously shielded from the health care system by the gate-
keeper GP, would benefit.

It is therefore not even necessary to invoke the horror scenarios,
predicting run-away demands on the NHS's resources, in order to
be sceptical about the proposition that dilemmas of choice can be
avoided. These scenarios fall into two categories. The first stresses
the expanding scope for, and cost of, medical intervention resulting
from technological innovation: for example, the introduction of
new drugs like interferon beta, which, it has been estimated (Walley
and Barton 1995) might alone add 10 per cent to the national drug
bill if used widely in the treatment of multiple sclerosis. The second
stress the exponential growth in public expectations, threatening an
ever widening gap between what is available and what is demanded
(Thwaites 1987). Even if such prophecies turn out to be exaggerated, there is every reason to expect that the management of scarce
resources will remain one of the defining characteristics of all health
care systems. In the two concluding chapters, we therefore turn to
examining whether, given that priority setting and rationing appear
to be inevitable, the process could be improved, starting with the
international experience.

9

WHAT CAN WE LEARN FROM OTHERS?

If dilemmas of choice in the allocation of resources are inevitable in the delivery of health care, and if therefore priority setting and rationing are inescapable, what criteria should be used, who should make the decisions and how should they be made? Interest in these questions is international: a reminder, as pointed out earlier, that the NHS does not have a monopoly of concern about the gap between supply and demand and that although its special characteristics may help to account for the form that priority setting and rationing have taken in Britain, they do not explain the necessity for doing so. In the first half of the 1990s a variety of countries, with very different health care systems, addressed the twin issues of how to decide between competing claims for scarce resources and what the limits of collective responsibility for the provision of health care should be. This chapter accordingly examines the international debate in order to see whether any general lessons can be distilled from the experience of the countries concerned, while the following, and concluding, chapter asks whether and how British policy and practice could be improved.

THE OREGON EXPERIMENT

The Oregon experiment not only was the first attempt to systematize rationing, and to base the allocation of resources on a set of explicit criteria, but it remains the only example of policy prescriptions being implemented in practice. And even though it has not been imitated elsewhere, the ideas which shaped it continue to influence debate. In the debate about rationing, it has gained almost mythical status. It is therefore worth examining in some detail, drawing on the large literature it has spawned – critical and otherwise. But before we do so, it is important to be clear about the context of the Oregon experiment. This was designed to tackle a problem specific to the United States: that of ensuring health care for the uninsured, i.e. a vulnerable and powerless minority. While this does not necessarily mean that the principles shaping the Oregon experiment are not transferable, it does suggest that there may be social and political constraints on the feasibility of adopting its approach in countries with universal health care coverage.

Funds for providing care of the uninsured in Oregon – as in the other American states – come from fixed budgets allocated for this purpose. These fiscal limits, as in the case of the NHS, set limits to what can be provided. The Oregon experiment has its origins in a case which gave dramatic expression to the implications of such limits (Kitzhaber and Kemmy 1995). This was the case of Coby Howard, a sort of first cousin to the case of child B in Britain. Coby Howard was a seven year old boy suffering from acute leukaemia and his one chance of survival, albeit a slim one, was thought to be bone marrow transplant. The State of Oregon refused to pay for this treatment; Coby Howard's parents turned to private fund-raising but he died before the sum required could be raised.

It was this which prompted Oregon's endeavour to devise a package of care to which all uninsured members of the population would be entitled. This was to be done by ranking different conditions and forms of treatment (what came to be known as condition/treatment pairs) in order of priority. The state legislature would then decide, in the light of what it was prepared to spend in total on the health care of the uninsured, where to draw the line in the hierarchy of priorities. Those conditions above the line would form part of the guaranteed package; those below the line would be excluded from it. The decision to adopt this strategy was taken in 1989 when the Oregon Basic Health Services Act was passed. Five years later, after much delay caused by opposition in Washington, the Oregon plan came into effect.

The task of defining the package of care – i.e. of defining the menu of health services to be provided – was carried out by a specially appointed commission. In approaching its work, the commission started off by taking two factors into account (Hadorn 1991; Garland 1992; Kaplan 1992). The first were community views. A series of meetings were organized to elicit the priorities attached by the population to broad categories of health (for example, the relative weight to be attached to the treatment of life threatening conditions as against preventive measures) and the weightings given to different values (such as equity, ability to function, quality and length of life, personal choice). On the basis of this exercise, modified in debate among the commissioners, a ranked list of categories of treatment was produced.

The second factor taken into account was the cost–benefit ratio of different forms of treatment, i.e. the relative cost of achieving specific outcomes. In the event, lack of adequate information, particularly about costs, persuaded the commission to abandon the cost–benefit formula. The formula was chiefly used, and then only in a watered down version, to rank condition/treatment pairs within the broad categories created by the commission: benefit, as measured on a quality of well-being scale, rather than cost appears to have been the main consideration in determining rankings. Lastly, in making their final decisions, the commissioners used a 'reasonableness test', taking into account such considerations as the public health impact, cost of medical treatment, incidence of condition, effectiveness of treatment, social costs and cost of non-treatment.

The rankings of the first list of 709 condition/treatment pairs by the commission produced some bizarre results and provoked much criticism. For example, cosmetic breast surgery was ranked higher than treatment for an open thigh fracture and tooth capping was ranked higher than appendectomy. The commissioners went back to the drawing board and produced a revised set of rankings. Whereas the original list had given top ranking to somewhat unusual conditions like phenylketonuria and candiasis, the new one gave highest priority to common conditions like pneumonia and tuberculosis. Organ transplants moved from near the bottom to near the middle of the list (Egan 1991). In 1991 the Oregon legislature decided to fund the top 587 condition/treatment pairs out of the total list of 709, voting extra money in order to provide the necessary funding. The conditions left out of Oregon's basic package were similar in character to those excluded by NHS from their purchasing plans, i.e. they tended to be treatment for minor conditions, futile care and services having little or no effect on care.

The Oregon plan appears to have succeeded in its objectives. It replaced one form of rationing (the exclusion of a section of the population from eligibility for health care funding) by another (restricting the services on offer). In doing so, it widened access to health care. The number of people with an entitlement to health care increased, while conversely the number of those relying on emergency services and charity care decreased (Kitzhaber and Kemmy 1995). In this respect, of course, it does not provide a model for countries like Britain, which already provide universal access. In what follows, therefore, our analysis concentrates on examining the Oregon plan as a model not for extending access but for taking decisions about the rationing process. Three characteristics of the Oregon plan, in particular, have a claim to attention in the consideration of its wider applicability. First, it represents a model of a particular type of rationing: by the explicit denial of certain forms of treatment or the exclusion of specific services. Second, it provides a model which seeks to achieve political legitimacy for such decisions by involving the community. Third, and linked to the previous two points, it is a model for giving visibility to the criteria used in reaching decisions about what to exclude. We consider each in turn.

Explicitness has, in itself, an intuitive appeal as a principle of rationing, a theme which will be further explored in the next, concluding chapter. It satisfies the requirement that, in a democratic society, all decisions must be capable of passing the test of public scrutiny. Lifting the veils is seen, from this perspective, to be desirable in its own right, which is why the Oregon experiment has been hailed in Britain as an example of letting the sunlight into the dark corners of paternalistic decision-making by professionals (Smith 1991b). But it is important to draw a distinction between the *general* argument for explicitness, the *specific* form it may take when applied to health care and the *consequences* that flow from adopting a particular model. And it was the *form* that the Oregon experiment took which attracted much subsequent criticism.

The first criticism is one to which all forms of rationing based on limiting the health care menu are vulnerable and which we encountered in Chapter 6 when examining the reaction to those health authorities in Britain which sought to follow this strategy. This is that patients are heterogeneous: variations in the effect of treatment on individuals within condition/treatment groups may be as large as variations between such groups (Klein 1991; Aaron 1992). The second criticism, which again applies to all forms of rationing by denial, is that the Oregon approach failed to disaggregate the notion of treatment. If the cost–benefit criterion is to be invoked, why limit its application to the selection of treatments? As Veatch (1992) has argued, in his comments on the Oregon experiment, taking as his example the case of appendectomy:

The real issue is not whether to perform the appendectomy; it is whether to fund the countless marginal interventions that are potentially part of the procedure – marginal blood tests and repeat tests; precautionary, preventive antibiotic therapy before surgery; the number of nurses in the operating room; the backup support on call or in the hospital. Even more decisions about marginal elements will arise during the recovery phase – exactly how many days of hospital stay are permitted, how often the physician should make rounds, how many follow-up tests there should be, and so on. Many of these are predicted to offer more benefits than harm, but with margins so small that one could argue that resources ought to be used elsewhere.

Whatever the strengths and weaknesses of the particular form of rationing adopted in Oregon, the state's strategy does appear to provide a recipe for giving democratic legitimacy to decisions about rationing. Not only did the Oregon legislature accept political responsibility for determining the final package of health care – although whether it would have done so if it had been for the population as a whole as distinct from a minority of the poor is another, ultimately unanswerable, question – but the process of generating the rankings involved, as we have seen, extensive community consultation. In this respect, however, the Oregon experiment provides a warning rather than an example. The community, it turned out, was reluctant to be involved. Only 600 citizens turned up at the meetings called to discuss priorities and, of these, 56 per cent worked in the health care system. 'In the absence of nonmedical popular or elite interest', Fox and Leichter (1991) have noted, 'the playing field was left largely to the medical experts'. In other words, an experiment which began with the presumption that decisions about rationing should not be left to doctors ended up with the profession taking the leading role.
  Turning to the third aspect of the Oregon experiment which has been held out as a model for imitation, the fact that it gave visibility to the criteria being used in making decisions about priorities, an agnostic assessment is again appropriate. The initial assumption that rankings could be determined by the use of technical instruments like the cost–benefit ratio of different treatments was, as we have seen, abandoned: not only was the required information lacking but its use led to some outcomes that invited ridicule (the

reason why appendectomy was ranked lower than tooth capping was that the greater medical benefits which it offered were outweighed by the lower cost of the latter). The way in which community values were translated into rankings was obscure: 'There is no reason to believe that a different set of commissioners, reacting to the same community meeting process, would have arrived at a similar ranking of services' (Daniels 1992). And the use of the 'reasonableness test' clearly allowed great scope for discretion in the way treatments were ranked. What had started out with the intention of being a highly transparent process turned out, in the event, to be highly impermeable.

It is therefore difficult to resist the conclusion drawn by one of the proponents of the Oregon experiment (Hadorn 1991):

> With regard to Oregon's (and other) efforts to set health care priorities, in the end, what may matter most is that the 'product' of priority setting efforts – whether a prioritized list, a set of guidelines, or some combination thereof – appears intuitively sensible. Absent a gold standard of validity, there can be no 'right' way to set health care priorities, nor any single 'correct' list or set of guidelines.

It is a conclusion which is reinforced when we examine, in the next section, the attempts of other countries to devise strategies for priority setting.

A CACOPHONY OF PRINCIPLES

The various government committees and commissions on priority setting that have reported in different countries over the past few years are a monument to perplexity. Their reports provide eloquent testimony to the difficulties involved in reaching anything like a consensus about the criteria, let alone a methodology, for deciding between competing claims and determining what should or should not be provided. In what follows no attempt will be made to review all these reports systematically or in depth (for surveys, see Abel-Smith *et al*. 1995; Ham 1995). The intention, rather, is to identify the main similarities and differences between the approaches adopted and to set out the main elements of the various strategies for priority setting that are on offer.

One theme running through most of the reports is unsurprising to anyone familiar with the rhetoric of the NHS in the 1990s. This is the invocation of the effectiveness criterion for screening out – or giving low priority to – those treatments where evidence is lacking that they make any difference to people's health. This is something of an illusionist's trick, as we have argued, insofar as it appears to offer a way of prioritizing without inflicting pain: of avoiding, or at least postponing, rationing in the strict sense, i.e. the denial of services that do work. No one, after all, can object to cutting out the waste implied by funding treatments that do not appear to produce a benefit or a health gain. The difficulty, as we saw in Chapter 8, is that most treatments do benefit *someone*, even if at a low level of probability, and that the real problem usually is one of selection. As in Britain again, there is therefore much emphasis internationally on the production of guidelines designed to target treatment on those patients most likely to benefit.

There is rather less agreement as to whether allocative efficiency - the principle that resources should be used to achieve the maximum benefit for society as a whole rather than for individual patients – should be a criterion. The Dutch (Dunning 1992) and New Zealand (National Advisory Committee on Core Health and Disability Services 1994) reports both stress efficiency or value for money as factors that should be taken into account when deciding on priorities. But neither proposes that this criterion should be used in an automatic fashion – i.e. that priority should go to those procedures or interventions which have the most favourable cost–benefit ratio – or commits itself to a formula (such as QALYs) for calculating the yield. To quote the cautious words of the New Zealand committee: 'there may be occasions where it is wise for public funds to provide a reasonably effective procedure for many people, rather than a more effective but very costly one which could only be made available to a few'.

In contrast, the Swedish report (Swedish Parliamentary Priorities Commission 1995) explicitly rejects the efficiency principle for deciding on priorities between programmes. 'Fair comparison of the effects is impossible', it argues. The cost–efficiency principle should therefore 'only be applied to the comparison of methods for treating the same illness'. It is therefore relevant at the level of clinical decision-making about individual patients rather than at the level of political decision-making about broad priorities between services. The following quote from the commission's report illustrates the implications of taking this view:

If resources are limited, then in certain situations it may be reasonable to opt for the second best treatment. In hip surgery, for example, a steel prosthesis is less expensive than a titanium one but less durable. It must be considered acceptable for a physician, as is often the case, to choose a steel prosthesis for a patient aged over 80 while giving a titanium one to a patient who is 70 years old and might perhaps need renewed surgery after a few years. In dealing with pronounced coronary strictures involving a risk of stroke, one can choose between surgery and medication. Surgery is a good deal more expensive, involves a short-term risk but is in the long term a more effective means of averting stroke. If resources are limited it may be justifiable to refrain from expanding surgical activities and to stick to medication – which is simple, inexpensive but less effective – instead.

In short, we are back to micro rationing at the point of service delivery, where the choice is not between who should be treated but how the treatment should be carried out: a choice which, inevitably, will have to be made by clinicians.

Even in those countries where the efficiency principle is invoked as a tool for deciding on priorities, however, there has been no attempt to adopt anything like the Oregon model of a systematic ranking of all conditions and treatments. The point can be illustrated by the cases of New Zealand and the Netherlands. In both countries, the impetus for setting up the relevant committees came from the perceived need to devise a basic package of health care to be guaranteed to everyone. In New Zealand, the intention was to define the core services which health authorities would be expected to purchase on behalf of their populations; in the Netherlands, the intention was to define the legal responsibilities of insurance schemes.

Neither committee came up with a list of exclusions. The New Zealand committee almost from the start rejected the concept of a core as a tightly defined list of services which must be purchased (Cummings 1994), and has made no attempt to define the health care menu. Even in the case of those conditions where normally low priority was given to treatment ranked, it acknowledged, there might well be individual circumstances where there might be strong arguments for providing it: for example, cosmetic surgery for a ballet dancer. Instead, the committee has concentrated on working with the medical profession to create consensus about the way in which resources should be used, in the circumstances of individual patients, and to develop explicit, national priority criteria for access to elective surgical procedures. At the same time, it has invested in a variety of community consultation exercises to elicit views about the values – such as fairness and accessibility – that should drive the allocation of resources (Edgar 1995).

The New Zealand committee is atypical in that it has a continuing existence: it can therefore view priority setting and implementation as an evolutionary process over time. The Dunning committee, in contrast, was more representative in being a one-off exercise: its task was done once it had reported. Like the New Zealand committee, however, it refused to define the contents or limits of a basic package of health care. Instead, it offered four criteria or tests which should apply for the inclusion of any type of care. First, is it necessary? Second, is it effective? Third, is it efficient? Fourth, is it a matter of individual, rather than community, responsibility? The committee adopted a community-orientated, rather than medical, definition of 'necessary care'. Necessary services were those which 'guarantee normal function as a member of the community or simply protect existence as a member'.

Illustratively only, the committee gave some examples of how its tests would apply to specific procedures or services. One was in vitro fertilization. This, it conceded, might be considered necessary from an individual point of view, and was reasonably cost-effective. But, it argued, IVF failed to pass the necessity test: 'Undesired childlessness in the Netherlands poses no danger to the community, and it cannot be said that childlessness interferes with normal function in our society'. Homeopathic medicine failed the effectiveness and efficiency tests and was, moreover, affordable to everyone: it should therefore not be included in any basic health care package and responsibility should be left to the individual.

Both these examples are, of course, familiar from our analysis of the purchasing plans of NHS health authorities. Indeed, all attempts to specify procedures that should be excluded from the health care menu seem to end with much the same list of mainly marginal procedures or treatments. Two further examples illustrate the point. As part of its 1995 health care reforms, the Spanish government sought to devise a guaranteed package of health care entitlements (Cabases 1995), in part to ensure that increasing regional devolution would not lead to inequities in access. The result was to define entitlements in terms of existing services. The main services explicitly excluded were plastic surgery not related to accidents, disease or congenital malformation, spa treatment and rest cures, sex change surgery and psychoanalysis and hypnosis.

The criteria of effectiveness and efficiency were only to be applied to the introduction of new procedures. Again, when the Province of Ontario in Canada reviewed entitlements to health care coverage in 1994, its list of exclusions was remarkably similar to those of British health authorities. They included reversal of vasectomies and sterilization, routine circumcision, removal of tattoos, repair of earlobes deformed by heavy earrings and IVF, except for women with complete fallopian tube blockage (Ontario Ministry of Health 1994).

This somewhat schematic analysis of the reports does not, of course, capture the small print of their arguments and proposals. Several other points require noting. First, the rule of rescue gets widespread support, if only by implication. Both the Swedish and the Norwegian (Norheim 1992) reports give first priority to the treatment of life-threatening acute disease. Second, there is much emphasis on the concept of social solidarity, i.e. that the commitments of the health care system should be shaped by a sense of collective responsibility for the well-being of its members. This ethical imperative leads the Swedish report, for example, to give high priority to 'severely and chronically ill patients, to patients with reduced autonomy and to terminal care'. Third, there is recognition that the criteria used to determine political and clinical priorities may diverge and that many resource allocation decisions are taken when deciding on the treatment of individual patients rather than when determining priorities between groups or services.

Overall, then, the experience of other countries echoes that of the NHS. Setting priorities or devising criteria for rationing turns out to be a peculiarly intractable endeavour, where practice lags behind rhetoric. There appears to be no generally acceptable technical fix, such as cost–benefit analysis, for resolving the dilemmas encountered. Similarly, there is nothing like a universal model: the various countries, as we have seen, are unanimous only in rejecting the Oregon prototype. A multiplicity of criteria, some of which are incompatible with each other, may be invoked, ranging from efficiency to equity. Different criteria may be used at different levels in the decision-making process. And even when seemingly precise criteria for choice are put forward, they may prove contestable when applied to particular cases: so, for example, the Dunning committee's assertion that childlessness does not interfere with normal functioning in society may be challenged on the grounds that in some instances it patently does so (Willigenburg 1993).

In considering whether and how the British system for deciding on the allocation of scarce resources could be made more coherent or rigorous – the theme of our concluding chapter – there is therefore no ready-made model waiting to be taken off the shelf. Some aspects of the strategies adopted by other countries may, of course, be suitable for adaptation to the British context. But the starting point for any such exercise in self-analysis and self-improvement must be an acknowledgement of the daunting complexity of the task. In this respect, the international evidence shows – reassuringly perhaps – the NHS is far from unique in finding the management of scarcity difficult and problematic.

10

POLICY OPTIONS FOR
THE FUTURE

The notion of the perfect whole, the ultimate solution, in which all good
things coexist, seems to me to be not merely unattainable – that is a truism
– but conceptually incoherent; I do not know what is meant by a harmony
of this kind. Some of the Great Goods cannot live together. That is a
conceptual truth. We are doomed to choose, and every choice may entail
an irreparable loss.

(Berlin 1991)

To demonstrate that the problem of priority setting and rationing in
health care is as intractable as it is universal can, all too easily, lead
to a sense of comfortable complacency. The British way of priority
setting and rationing may be a case study of a system that puts
pragmatism before principles, that veils the decision-making process and that diffuses responsibility among various actors at different levels. But what if such 'muddling through elegantly' (D.
Hunter 1991) is the best that can be done? What if the search for a
model of decision-making that will resolve conflicts about the
criteria that should be used in allocating scarce resources is a quest
for the chimera?

Furthermore, what if a dim half light is preferable to bright
sunshine when it comes to certain types of decision-making? Explicitness in decision-making is not, after all, an absolute value
overriding all other considerations. Health care, more than perhaps
any other service, forces 'tragic choices' (Calabresi and Bobbit
1978), i.e. decisions that determine who shall live and who shall die.
The treatment of end stage renal failure is a classic case in point.
The opacity of the process by which political decisions about the
allocation of resources (priorities) become transformed in the NHS
into clinical decisions about who should be treated (rationing) may

therefore have a useful social function by taking some of the pain and sense of collective guilt out of such 'tragic choices'. Perhaps, therefore, the NHS's way of doing things represents a sensible accommodation to the inevitable, as well as being a reflection of the wider political culture which gave birth to it: a paternalist culture characterized by suspicion of written constitutions and abstract principles.

But this is too easy a conclusion: a nagging sense of unease remains. To explain why a particular system has developed in a particular way, and why it may be in the self-interest of many of the actors involved to maintain it, does not necessarily justify its perpetuation. At the political level of priority setting, 'muddling through' may simply become a pretext for blame avoidance: a way of fudging responsibility in the hope of diverting attention from the gap between what can be done and what the available resources allow to be done. At the service delivery end of rationing, clinical discretion may veil not only uncertainty but arbitrariness and arrogance in decision-making: resources may go to the most persuasive patients or to those who are seen as most acceptable and interesting (Maxwell 1995). And many of the choices that are made cannot be described as 'tragic'. Indeed, by concentrating on dramatic examples of decisions involving matters of life and death we risk distorting priorities by ignoring those services which provide care for those who cannot be cured.

Moreover, there are signs that some of the foundations on which the system is built may be crumbling. Medical paternalism is no longer accepted unquestioningly; the medical profession itself is beginning to resent having to accept responsibility for rationing scarce resources. Finally, the NHS now no longer has the defining characteristic that made the wartime rationing of food and clothing acceptable: universality. Wartime rationing, as we saw in Chapter 1, was seen as fair because it applied to everyone, rich and poor alike. But in the case of health care, the private sector offers an escape route to those who can afford it. Unlike the black market, it is socially acceptable. And in recent decades, it has grown rapidly: while private practice was very much a fringe activity in the early days of the NHS, now more than one-fifth of the population is covered by insurance. The NHS's principle of allocating resources according to need is therefore challenged by the private sector, which supplies according to demand. In deciding whether or not to offer treatment, consultants therefore use different criteria in their private practice from those they apply when making decisions in the context of their NHS work. It is a situation calculated to inspire cynicism about clinical judgement.

In addressing this sense of disquiet, and in trying to draw out some prescriptive conclusions from the evidence analysed in previous chapters, it is helpful to draw a distinction between two ways of conceiving decision-making: Plato's and Aristotle's (Beiner 1983). The first way is to see decision-making as a search for an ideal solution which, once discovered, will then provide all the answers, resolving the conflicts between different criteria and values. It is because this approach is as inappropriate as it is unachievable in the case of allocating scarce resources in health care – if only because so many competing criteria can be invoked, as we saw in Chapter 3 – that it is all too easy to adopt an attitude of resigned scepticism.

The other way is to see decision-making as deliberation and dialogue, as an exercise in making judgements based not on science but on practical wisdom. From this perspective, it is the quality of the deliberation and dialogue that is critical. The search is not for the 'right' solution – the magic machine that, once found, will then crank out decisions automatically – but for the appropriate process of deliberation. The test is not whether the debate will ever yield conclusions that can end argument for all time – an unattainable aim – but whether it is being conducted appropriately. Adopting this approach allows us to develop criteria for assessing the way in which decisions about priority setting and rationing are made. We can ask whether the available information is adequate to allow judgements to be made. We can ask whether the process of decision-making allows sufficient opportunities for all the parties involved to engage in the dialogue.

In addition, there are some questions specific to the case of the NHS, arising from the way in which it is organized. The NHS – like all services funded out of taxation – is accountable to Parliament, through the Secretary of State, for the way it allocates and spends public money. The process of taking decisions about priorities and rationing must therefore satisfy the requirements of public accountability (Day and Klein 1987). The Secretary of State has to be able to justify the decisions taken in his or her name. Further, and following on from this, the NHS is also accountable to the collectivity at large, in the weaker but no less important sense of the word, of having a duty to explain and justify its decisions in public: so if there is a case for implicit rationing (as indeed there is) then this has to be explicitly argued. We therefore have to ask whether the present process of reaching decisions about priorities and rationing satisfies the requirement of transparency.

These, then, are the questions around which this chapter is organized: our starting point being, to quote Albert Weale's (1990) elegant formulation, that while general principles are not very helpful in determining priorities or rationing decisions, because of the latter's complexity and contingency on particular circumstances, 'the basic structure of resource allocating institutions is something to which general principles can be applied'. We begin by examining the adequacy of the available information, before moving on to the processes by which decisions are taken.

To avoid confusion, two definitional points must be borne in mind throughout our discussion. First, to reiterate, there is the distinction between priority setting (the allocation of resources to particular services or programmes) and rationing (the allocation of resources within these budgetary envelopes to individual patients at the point of service delivery). The same considerations do not necessarily apply to both. Second, in what follows we start from the assumption that both priority setting and rationing are about the dilemmas of choice that remain *after* 'waste' has been eliminated. No one can quarrel with the proposition that the NHS should cut out spending on procedures or treatments that are not effective, although translating it into practice raises all sorts of problems. But, as we have argued, this is at best a way of attenuating or postponing the dilemmas of choice and at worst an illusionist's trick for making difficult decisions disappear – temporarily.

THE INFORMATION REQUIREMENTS

One conclusion emerged clearly and strongly from the review of purchasing plans in Chapter 5. This is that at present very few, if any, health authorities provide the information required to assess, debate or challenge their decisions about priorities. If the purchasing plans are supposed to be the window through which the evidence and rationale for the priority decisions of the commissioning authorities are made visible to the outside world, they fail (with very few exceptions) in this function. The window is frosted. This reflects as much ignorance as a deliberate attempt to veil the decision-making process: even the members of the authorities, as they themselves concede, lack much of the required information.

Yet it is not difficult to specify the kind of information required. On the supply side, we need to know how the existing resources of health authorities are distributed and what the level of services provided is, in terms of accessibility and availability. On the demand side, we need to know the extent to which supply falls short of national norms and local evidence about need. In other words, we should be able to translate resource provision into a picture of who gets what and to compare what is on offer in a particular district with what is available elsewhere. Without such a systematic, overall review, it is difficult to see how particular shortfalls can be identified: surely a necessary preliminary step before deciding on priorities between competing claims on resources.

The failure so far of most health authorities to provide information of this kind can largely be explained, as we have argued, by their lack of expertise, the poor quality or ambiguity of much of the available data and the many pressures on their managerial capacity. But while it is possible to explain past failure, this does not justify accepting it as inevitable in the future. If we accept the principle that priority setting should involve dialogue – and that such a dialogue should, further, be able to draw on publicly available information – then the availability of a comprehensive picture is a necessary condition. Indeed, in the absence of a *comprehensive* picture the danger is that the selective availability of evidence will in itself bias perceptions and distort priorities.

So, for example, the visibility of information about waiting lists and times for elective surgery – and the consequent political salience of this issue – has, in itself, tended to drive national and local priorities. Further, much of the available information may reflect the self-interest of providers, individual consultants or pressure groups engaged in drumming up support for their particular services by identifying inadequacies: a particularly persuasive strategy when visible lives are at risk. If the production of information is the result of a competition to give visibility to particular claims on resources, then any decisions about priorities based on such information is likely to be biased accordingly. Services with low visibility are likely to get low priority; hence the case for providing the contextual information required to compare different claims on resources.

But to make this point is to raise a further, more troubling issue: the currency of comparison. This, as we have seen, perplexes health authorities. They use a multiplicity of criteria when assessing competing claims on resources. Some, like health gains, tend to be somewhat nebulous. Others may conflict with each other. What information is required when moving from the identification of the competing claims on resources to choosing between them? Enter the economists. Here the claim is that 'The economic evaluation of alternative diagnostic and therapeutic interventions is not merely a help to the processes by which decision makers allocate scarce economic resources, it is an essential ingredient' (Maynard and Bloor 1995). Indeed, economists tend to equate rationality in decision-making with the use of economic techniques of analysis. Therefore, should systematic economic evaluation form part of the specifications for any basic information requirements for purchasers? Should purchasers be required to specify the 'yield' of different investment options?

Economic evaluation comes in many forms. There is cost–effectiveness analysis, which consists of comparing the cost–benefit ratio of different interventions designed to achieve the same outcomes (Robinson 1993). There is programme budgeting and marginal analysis (PBMA), which consists of comparing the benefits offered both by existing services and by new bids for extra resources (Donaldson 1995). There is the QALY technique, which compares different forms of intervention and treatment on a common numeraire: the cost per life year, adjusted for quality, yielded by any given intervention. And so on.

It is well beyond the scope of this chapter, as well as the competence of the authors, to review these techniques in any detail. But some common problems need to be noted. They are all dependent on information about outcomes, which may not be available or, if available, may be inaccurate or even misleading. For example, outcomes may be contingent, to return to a point made earlier, on the conditions under which a particular study is carried out. If the selection of patients is sufficiently rigorous – with an eye to picking only those who are likely to survive for a long time – then the outcomes will be accordingly favourable. But this says little about likely outcomes if the criteria of selection are relaxed and if less expert clinicians carry them out as they become more widely adopted. Equally, these techniques raise the question of how future benefits should be valued: what time span should be involved and how discount rates should be calculated (Sheldon 1992). Finally, there is the problem that calculations are based on information about groups. Radically different conclusions might therefore follow if those groups were disaggregated and resources were concentrated on those patients most likely to benefit.

The QALY-type approach raises some additional difficulties. It has been criticized from a variety of perspectives. There are technical problems about deriving weightings for the quality of life from survey data. There is the difficulty of applying the technique to groups like the mentally handicapped (Crisp 1991). There is the fear that using QALY-type information will discriminate against the elderly, since they will usually have fewer life years ahead of them following a successful intervention than the young – even though the quality of those years may be high. Many of these criticisms may be dispelled as the techniques for calculating QALYs become more sophisticated. But technical refinement – as in the case of formulae for calculating the allocation of resources to local or health authorities – carries its own danger: mystification. Unless all those engaged in debating and discussing priorities fully understood the assumptions incorporated in the process of calculating QALYs – and the often dubious foundation of evidence on which they are based – the risk is that they might mislead rather than inform (Spiegelhalter *et al*. 1992).

In any case, the usefulness of QALY-type calculations for decisions about priorities may be more limited than their advocates concede. Consider the following figures of the cost per QALY, at 1990 prices, of competing therapies: £270 for GP advice to stop smoking, £1180 for hip replacement, £4710 for a kidney transplant, £7840 for a heart transplant, £14,150 for cholesterol treatment and therapy and £18,830 for home haemodialysis (Maynard 1994). Some broad conclusions do indeed follow from figures such as these. Funding GP advice to smokers is clearly a good buy; kidney transplants are to be preferred to haemodialysis; cholesterol screening is a very expensive way of saving lives. Many of these conclusions might, indeed, follow from less elaborate techniques of analysis. But a health authority, unless composed of card-carrying utilitarians, is unlikely to cut back its budget for kidney transplants (say) in order to free funds for hip replacements, let alone GP advice to smokers.

In both theory (Chapter 3) and practice (Chapter 5) a variety of criteria can be used – and are used – in making decisions about priorities. The language of priorities – to reiterate one of the main themes running through this book – is inevitably a pluralistic one. This is not to decry the role of economic analysis. It clearly has an important role in drawing attention to the opportunity costs of investing in different treatments or services, in stressing benefits to the community as a whole rather than to individuals and in forcing a disciplined comparison of alternative ways of spending money. It thus provides an important input into the decision-making process. But in doing so, it illuminates the dilemmas of choice rather than resolving them. It is better at forcing people to address questions which they might otherwise prefer to ignore – about, for example, the wisdom of spending a large sum on saving individual lives rather than spreading it around on less visible or dramatic activities – than at answering them. It is therefore difficult to conclude that economic analysis – certainly at this stage in its development – should form part of a required part of any basic information package for decision-making.

ASKING THE PUBLIC

There appears to be a general consensus that one of the inputs into the decision-making process about priorities should be information about the views of the public. The Department of Health, as we have seen, has been strongly promoting the notion of public involvement in decisions about priorities; the Health Committee of the House of Commons (1995) further endorsed this principle in its report on priority setting in the NHS. And if health authorities are to be responsive to local preferences when framing their purchasing plans, then clearly they have to elicit the views of the populations that they serve.

The notion of 'the public' is, of course, problematic. There are many different publics. The interests and views of the users of NHS services may, for example, be rather different from those of the population at large. In turn, the population at large may split into geographical or social groups, each with their special preoccupations. Nevertheless, undeterred by such considerations, health authorities have responded to the Department of Health's exhortations, if with a varying degree of enthusiasm. There has been a proliferation of public consultation exercises, using a variety of methods. These include population surveys, public meetings, focus groups and panels meeting over time (Redmayne 1995, 1996). Not only do the methods of these exercises differ. So, too, do the aims. For two rather different strategies seem to underlie the various attempts at eliciting public preferences. The first is to ask the public to rank its preferences: to prioritize between different claims on resources. The second is to ask the public about its own priorities for improvements in services: to elicit views about what are perceived to be the most urgent needs from the perspective of the population being served. While the former seeks to tap people's general perceptions or values about the NHS's priorities as citizens, the latter seeks to tap their experience as actual or potential consumers.

Over time the emphasis seems to have switched from the first to the second strategy: from viewing public consultation as a kind of referendum about the NHS's priorities, and the values that should guide decision-makers, to seeing it as an exercise in consumer research. Nor is this surprising. There are both theoretical and practical problems about the first type of strategy. On grounds of theory, it is difficult to know what weight to attach to free floating opinions which are neither the product of debate nor anchored in knowledge. Such instant exercises in direct democracy carry the risk, as Hunter (1993) has put it, 'of establishing a dictatorship of the uninformed'. If we see democracy as being reason-respecting rather than want-regarding (Weale 1990), as being about open deliberation rather than preference aggregation, then there seems every reason for scepticism about this kind of approach. There may be ways of overcoming this particular kind of objection: so, for example, the use of citizen juries has been advocated (Fishkin 1991) as a means of engaging a representative sample of the population in informed deliberation. But, as yet, little is known about the stability of the opinions produced by this method.

There are also practical problems – reinforcing theoretical scepticism – about trying to elicit the views of the public about the values that should guide decisions about priorities, particularly by the use of surveys. The questions may produce inconsistent answers. Consider the answers to the following two questions asked in a national survey (*Daily Telegraph* 12 September 1994). The first asked respondents whether they agreed with the statement: 'Whoever they are, and whatever the causes of their illness, every ill person should always have the right to the best treatment as quickly as possible'. The second asked them whether they agreed with the statement: 'People who bring their illnesses on themselves – by, for example, smoking or drinking heavily – should be lower down in the queue for NHS care than other patients'. The two are, clearly, incompatible with each other. But while 96 per cent agreed with the first statement, 41 per cent also agreed with the second statement.

This example demonstrates the difficulty of framing appropriate questions and underlines the sensitivity of the answers to the precise phrasing used. Compounding this difficulty is the problem of how choices between different claims on resources should be expressed. Should people be asked to rank their preferences in terms of services (acute versus mental illness), groups of people (the old versus the young) or specific treatments (heart transplants versus treatment for infertility)? Or should people be asked about the relative priority that should be attached to health care that prolongs life and reduces pain and disability as against health care that prevents illness?

Such problems may make it very difficult to interpret the results of surveys and to translate the views elicited from surveys into decisions about resource allocation. One of the most sophisticated of such exercises (Bowling 1993) involved both group discussions and a public opinion survey in one health district. Of those interviewed, 63 per cent agreed (13 per cent of them strongly) with the statement that 'Services which deal with mental illness are at least as important as those which deal with physical illness'. But mental illness services emerged only tenth in the priority ranking of services, behind treatment for children with life-threatening illnesses like leukaemia (in first place), special care and pain relief for people who are dying (second), high technology surgery and procedures like heart transplants that treat life-threatening conditions (third) and medical research (fourth).

These kind of exercises fail to capture, in short, the complexity of decisions about resource allocations. Priorities are seldom absolute. To give top priority to the treatment of children with life-threatening conditions like leukaemia does not necessarily mean giving it overriding priority over other claims: it involves balancing – as in the case of child B – cost against the probability of success, as well as taking other factors (like the suffering involved) into account. It may be that other methods, like discussion groups (Bowie *et al.* 1995), can address such complexities better than surveys. But this remains an open question.

The development of more sophisticated methodologies may, as in the case of economic analysis, resolve some of these doubts. But some more fundamental difficulties about deriving priorities from the view of the public remain. It cannot be assumed that public priorities are homogeneous. Most studies provide no information about either the distribution of views within any given population or the intensity with which those views are held. Yet this can be very important for a health authority in its decision-making process. How, for example, should diffuse, low key support for a policy of concentrating resources in one facility be weighed against concentrated passionate support for a local hospital threatened with closure?

Further, public priorities differ from those of the health service professionals. While the public gave first priority to the treatment of children with life-threatening conditions, in the study quoted above GPs put it in fifth place; conversely, GPs gave first ranking to community services at home, while the public put these in fifth place. The same conclusion emerges from another study (Heginbotham 1993), which asked a sample of the public, doctors and managers to prioritize between a somewhat different list of services. Everyone agreed in putting childhood immunization first, but there was a sharp difference between the three groups when it came to heart transplants: the public put this in fifth place, while both doctors and managers ranked it ninth.

Similarly, there may be conflict between the views of the public and other evidence. As we have seen, advice on stopping smoking appears to be one of the most cost-effective ways of using NHS resources. But at least one study (Richardson *et al*. 1992) suggests that this is seen as a very low priority by the public: only 8 per cent of the public interviewed thought that help for those who want to stop smoking was important.

It is therefore not surprising that public opinion is seldom reflected directly in the decisions of health authorities about resource allocations. Our case studies suggest that the results of such consultation exercises are used to legitimate strategies already being followed rather than leading to any changes. This may be inevitable, since such exercises are only one of the many inputs into the decision-making process. Moreover, given the ambiguities of many of the responses, it is not self-evident what weight should be given to the views of the public as against other, possibly conflicting, evidence about effectiveness and considerations like the feasibility of switching resources. This is no doubt why there has been a retreat from such exercises in direct democracy and a move towards more conventional consumer research. If people complain about problems of access to services on the basis of their own experience, as they do, this is likely to carry more weight than if they are asked to rank priorities in questionnaires. And the evidence of the purchasing plans, which put much emphasis on decentralizing services in order to facilitate local access, confirms that it is this kind of input which influences policy.

In any case, the public appears to be less enthusiastic about being consulted about priorities than the zeal of health authorities in conducting consultation exercises might suggest. For while the results of the various surveys that have been conducted convey a babble of messages, depending largely on the way in which they ask their questions, they agree on one point. This is that people believe that it is doctors – not they, NHS managers or the government – who should be responsible for deciding on priorities. There is, therefore, no strong case for arguing that the strategy of asking the public about priorities should be pursued more vigorously. In any case, it raises a troubling issue. The justification for following it is that local priorities should reflect local circumstances: that health authorities should be responsive to the populations that they serve. But this prompts a wider, and more fundamental, question: what should be the relationship between national and local decision-making about priorities? We address this question in the next section.

NATIONAL VERSUS LOCAL PRIORITIES

There is an unresolved tension at the heart of the relationship between national and local decision-making – between the centralization of credit and the diffusion of blame – about priorities. Not only is the Secretary of State accountable to Parliament for the way in which NHS resources are used but, as the flood of guidelines about priorities pouring out from the NHS Executive shows, the centre plays a highly directive role. A case in point is the setting of targets for waiting lists and the number of specific procedures that should be carried out. At the same time, however, the Secretary of State firmly puts responsibility for taking decisions about priorities on to the health authorities at the periphery. The point is well caught in the following attempt by a former Secretary of State (Bottomley 1994) to define the position:

> We can set only the framework in which local decisions are made: clinicians and managers must determine the health needs of the local population and how they are best met. These decisions are given legitimacy when the views of patients and local needs are taken into account. . . . It is not the government's role to lay down local priorities or make local decisions; local purchasers and providers of health care are best placed to do that.

The government's response to the report on priorities of the Health Committee of the House of Commons (Secretary of State for Health 1995) attempted a further elaboration. It set out the 'key principles' that should guide local decisions about priorities. These were equity, efficiency and responsiveness.

If the achievement of equity, efficiency and responsiveness could be measured, then there might be no contradiction at the heart of the Department of Health's stance. The priorities of health authorities could be assessed in terms of their success in meeting these criteria, never mind the fine print of their resource allocation policies. But the department has yet to tell the world how it assesses the implementation of the three principles. Similarly, if performance could be measured in terms of outcomes – the impact on the population's health – then, again, it would be possible to reconcile the demands of accountability with giving health authorities scope for deciding on their priorities in their own way. But health outcomes are, as previously pointed out, mostly outside the control of the NHS.

There is a further problem. Equity, as we have seen, is a complex and ambiguous concept. And compounding complexity and ambiguity is the question of whether it should be applied locally or globally. In other words, does equity require that everyone should be entitled to the same mix and level of services regardless of where he or she lives, or does it simply require that all members of the population of a specific health authority should be entitled to equality of access for any given need? This is not a theoretical quibble. The case of IVF provides an example of a procedure which is available in some health authorities but not in others. Yet there is little evidence that such decisions reflect differences in need as distinct from the strength of local pressure, particularly from consultants: it therefore represents a particular kind of responsiveness, and it is far from clear whether this is what the Department of Health has in mind when evoking the notion.

Similarly, the wide variations in the rate of surgery for cataracts, hip replacements and coronary artery by-pass surgery suggest that global equity in access to treatment has not been achieved. Yet the Department of Health's interest in these variations seems to reflect less concern about equity than the hope that they allow scope for saving money by reducing activity at the top end of the range.

All this would seem to point towards a simple conclusion. This is that the Department of Health should explicitly set out what people are entitled to expect from the NHS (Lenaghan 1995). This would follow the logic of the Patient's Charter by setting out standards not just for waiting times but also for the availability of specific services. National priorities would thus be translated into expectations 'about the range and quality of care that a sample of average citizens, taken at random at different stages of life, can legitimately expect to receive from the health care system' (Weale 1995). Such a list of entitlements would, of course, also define the limits of the NHS's responsibilities: that is, the list would be as significant for what it excluded as for what it included.

Here, then, would appear to be the formula for ensuring transparency and openness. Ministers would be clearly accountable for delivering the entitlements; the long divorce between responsibility for setting the budget limits and responsibility for delivery of services would be ended. If ministers thought that the budget would not stretch to doing everything that they thought desirable, they would have to decide on the priorities between competing claims. No longer would they be able to indulge their imagination when sending out notes of guidance to health authorities, leaving it to them to match resources to words. The era of fudging and muddling through would be over.

Alas, for reasons explored in earlier chapters, the vision is as delusive as it is enticing. The notion of defining a menu of health care entitlements ignores complexity and uncertainty, the heterogeneity of patients, the substitutability of services and the pace of change in medical technology (Klein 1994). The real issue, as we have seen, is not so much which services or types of care should be on offer but which patients should be selected for what kinds of treatment and at what level of intensity. It is therefore difficult to disagree with the government's conclusion, in its response to the Health Committee's priority report, that 'No one list could ever hope to accommodate the range and complexity of the different cases which individual clinicians face all the time'.

Once again, therefore, the attempt to find a formula which will solve for all time the problem of priority setting fails. Once again, too, we are left to consider how we can improve the *process* of debate. There are a variety of options. One such would be to institutionalize the debate by creating a body charged specifically with this task. So, for example, the Royal College of Physicians (1995) has proposed the creation of a National Council for Health Care Priorities. The aim of such a council would be:

> to find ways and methods for improving priority setting in the NHS, bearing in mind the need to involve, educate and inform

the public, the professions and the government. It would have the practical function of examining the evidence relating to resource allocation in health care . . . and it would review the basis and methods for determining allocations and their implication. Its role in society would be to identify all the relevant issues, analyse them publicly and comprehensively, and satisfy all the interested parties that their views are being considered.

The advantages of such an approach, like those of the New Zealand model, are twofold. It conceives of priority setting as a continuous process rather than as a search for a once-and-for-all solution and it acknowledges the pluralism of both values and interests that are involved.

Another option, not necessarily incompatible with the creation of a National Council for Health Care Priorities, is to make better use of existing institutions: to put some flesh on the doctrine of parliamentary accountability. While repudiating responsibility for the substantive priority decisions taken by health authorities, the Department of Health has conceded that these are accountable to the centre for the way in which they take those decisions. There is therefore no reason why the House of Commons Health Committee should not demand regular reports on how the department – through the NHS Executive and its regional offices – discharges the task of ensuring that decisions about priorities are taken with due regard for the three principles of equity, efficiency and responsiveness. How are these principles interpreted when assessing the performance of health authorities? And what action is taken if these fail to pass the test?

Similarly, there is good reason for arguing that the NHS Executive should be required to put a price on its own priorities: that when guidelines are published, requiring health authorities to take action, the cost implications should be spelt out. Such a step might help to ensure that priority aspirations do not outrun financial resources: that the temptations of political expediency do not inflate the list of rhetorical priorities. And it would force debate about the trade-off between priorities: the relative weight to be attached to different claims on resources.

But while the searchlight of parliamentary scrutiny could help to illuminate the relationship between the centre and the periphery, and to identify more clearly responsibility for decision-making about priorities, this only answers half the problem. There remains the issue of the wider accountability of health authorities to the communities that they serve. The next section therefore addresses this issue.

LOCAL ACCOUNTABILITY

Let us imagine, heroic and implausible though it may seem to make such an assumption, that health authorities have achieved the managerial and technical competence to produce purchasing plans that satisfy our ideal model of priority setting. They have provided a benchmark picture of what the authority's money is currently buying and for whom; they have set out the evidence about unmet needs and frustrated demands; they have, moreover, devised some clear-cut criteria for assessing the different claims on resources; they have even called on economists to supply cost–benefit analyses of the options. They have furthermore, as exhorted by the Department of Health, consulted widely. Would our requirement that priorities should be the product of open debate and dialogue be satisfied?

A nagging doubt would surely still remain. The production of more and better information – even a clearer exposition of the choices being faced – would still leave unresolved the question of the distribution of the opportunities for challenging decisions. There would still be an imbalance between the different actors in the health care arena: between, to return to a distinction made earlier, concentrated interests, notably providers, and diffuse interests. The former are organized and equipped to make use of the available information; the latter are not. Providing more and better information, in short, may not be a sufficient condition – although it may be a necessary one – for adequate debate and dialogue unless there are appropriate institutional mechanisms.

It is this kind of doubt which has prompted some (for example, Harrison and Hunter 1994) to argue that the only way to give legitimacy to local decisions about priorities is for them to be taken by elected bodies: to transfer responsibility for running health services to local government. There are obvious problems about this, notably that local government lacks the financial capacity for funding health care. But even waving these aside, there are grounds for scepticism. There is little evidence that elected local authorities have engaged in the kind of debate and dialogue about priorities that, we have argued, should characterize the NHS. This is despite the fact that, as we saw in Chapter 2, they face very similar problems in prioritizing between different claims on resources in the services which they run. On the contrary, they have tended to assume that the very fact of being elected bodies gives automatic legitimacy to whatever they decide: that there is no requirement on them to justify their decision-making processes. In contrast, health authorities – precisely because of their uncertainty about their legitimacy – have made much greater efforts to open up the processes by which they reach their decisions.

There remains one further possibility. This is for local government to adopt the role of scrutiny which Parliament plays at the national level, perhaps more effectively. There is, after all, no reason why local authorities should not set up committees charged with examining, and responding to, the priority decisions of health authorities, thus giving voice to the diffused interests of the population being served. The case for moving in this direction would be all the stronger if, as the Commission for Local Democracy (Jenkins 1995c) has suggested, the future lies in having directly elected chief executives with councillors concentrating on scrutinizing and monitoring the framing of policy and its implementation.

RATIONING AND THE ROLE OF DOCTORS

So far in this chapter we have concentrated on the political processes of setting priorities. We conclude by returning to the issue of rationing in the strict sense: the way in which professionals determine, within the constraints set by the decisions about priorities, the allocation of resources to individual patients. Should we be seeking to strip the veils off the process by which clinicians and other health care professionals decide on who gets what at the point of service delivery?

The present situation, of unfettered discretion, is in many ways unsatisfactory for both professionals and patients. For professionals, there is the tension between their roles as advocates and allocators. Real anguish may, in some cases, be involved in deciding between the claims of individual patients and the claims of the community at large. For patients, there is the fear that clinical decisions may be taken arbitrarily or even influenced by the doctor's wish to drum up custom for his or her private practice. Moreover, acceptance of implicit rationing depends crucially on trust in the medical profession. And there is some evidence (Mechanic 1995) that there has been erosion of trust: direct access by consumers to information about the options for treatment, often highlighted by the media, makes it less likely that decisions will be accepted unquestioningly.

The case for accepting implicit rationing remains, however. It is based, as we have seen, on the nature of the decision-making process in the encounter between doctor and patient. Again, we are back to uncertainty, complexity and the problem of applying general rules to specific patients in particular circumstances. The result may, indeed, be to shield decision-makers at the political levels from the consequences of their funding policies. But undesirable though this may be, the alternatives seem to be more undesirable still.

In one respect, though, this conclusion requires modification. The trend, as we have seen, has increasingly been to the mass production of guidelines. In devising these the medical profession is defining the criteria of good practice, including those for the selection of patients and for the appropriate level of treatment. In effect, this is a process which – potentially at least – could give visibility to the criteria being used in allocating resources.

It is not clear whether guidelines, as at present designed, would lend themselves to this purpose. Indeed, the process of producing them seems to be somewhat anarchic and we lack any systematic review of what they imply for the way in which NHS resources are used. There may be a case therefore to follow the example of Australia by devising guidelines for the development of guidelines, which specify who should take part in their formulation and the main elements that they should incorporate – including economic and epidemiological analysis (Lapsley 1995). Similarly, there is a case for following the example of New Zealand by developing national criteria for the selection of patients from waiting lists. And the same point applies to local protocols, which, as we saw in the case of IVF, may often incorporate moral or social judgements as well as professional ones.

Overall, then, the strategy could be to make the criteria of micro rationing more explicit, without attempting to constrain the discretion of individual clinicians and other health care professionals in the process of implementing them. It would imply making the medical profession collectively more accountable for the way in which rationing decisions are taken at the point of service delivery, while leaving it to the profession to hold its members to account for the way in which they interpret the collective decisions: this, after all, should be one of the purposes of clinical audit, institutionalized by the 1991 reforms of the NHS.

If this strategy were to be implemented it would mean, in turn, accepting that there will be variations in the way criteria are applied, reflecting the varying characteristics of both the professional and the patients concerned. To an extent it might be possible to deal with the consequent risk of unreasonableness (or incompetence) by making it easier for patients to ask for a second opinion and to have decisions reviewed, so providing a safeguard against the abuse of professional power by individual clinicians. But, as we saw in Chapter 2, discretion in the interpretation of guidelines, codes or rules characterizes all systems of service delivery. It would therefore be delusory to imagine that the NHS – alone among all such systems – will be able to solve the problem: the danger, rather, is that the attempt to do so might create an expensive bureaucracy without succeeding in its aim, while in the process eroding the morale and dedication of the professionals.

Some of the issues and difficulties in moving towards more explicit criteria are illustrated by the case of continuing care. This raises, in a particularly sharp form, the question of the limits of the health care system's responsibilities: the appropriate division of labour in long-term care – especially for elderly people – between the NHS and the social services. It has been a contentious issue throughout the history of the NHS but was given extra salience by the 1991 reforms. Accordingly, in 1995 the Department of Health asked health authorities to set out the criteria to be used in defining eligibility for continuing health care. In the event, most of the criteria lacked both precision and transparency: they said little more than 'that you are entitled to NHS continuing care if a doctor says so' (Saper and Laing 1995). So we are back to professional discretion. However, in the case of continuing care, there is to be an appeal procedure. Given some experience of how this new system is working, it may be possible to draw some conclusions about the scope for building on this precedent and extending the opportunities for having clinical decisions reviewed.

The example of continuing care also points up a danger. This is that by concentrating on trying to control clinical discretion in the selection and treatment of individual patients, we may overlook other forms of rationing which do not necessarily hinge on the way in which doctors allocate resources. As we saw in Chapter 1, rationing can take many forms. Some are more amenable to being made explicit than others. It is, as noted in Chapter 8, easier to develop guidelines for the selection of patients for surgery than it is to develop criteria for defining appropriate or adequate standards of care for those suffering from complex, chronic conditions. We have to be as alert to the problem of rationing by dilution (or by neglect) in services for those who cannot be cured as we are to the problem of rationing by the denial (or delay) of treatment in services which attract attention precisely because they offer either to save lives or to transform their quality.

Our analysis of the scope for making rationing more explicit therefore leads to much the same conclusion as our analysis of the scope for improving the process of priority setting. The notion that there is some 'ultimate solution', waiting to be discovered, is illusory. Decisions about managing scarce resources in the NHS – as elsewhere – involve trying to reconcile competing values, interests and concepts of the good. The balance struck at any one point in time will inevitably shift in the light of experience and changing social expectations. Neither science nor economics will resolve the pain of choice. The best we can hope for is to strive to improve the process by which we reach the decisions.

APPENDIX

Health authorities where one or more treatments are specifically excluded (except for overriding clinical reasons).

Procedure	Number of health authorities 1995/6 (n = 23)	Number of health authorities 1996/7 (n = 26)
IVF/GIFT	6	11
Dilation and curettage in women under 40	6	5
Tubal surgery	1	1
Cosmetic varicose vein surgery	6	8
Alternative/complementary therapies	3	5
Reversal female sterilization	9	15
Reversal male vasectomy	9	10
Grommets for glue ear in children	2	2
Sex change operations	8	11
Orthodontic interventions		
Prophylactic extraction of third molars	1	1
Asymptomatic impacted wisdom teeth	2	3
Dental implants	5	5
Extraction of deciduous teeth	1	1
Apicectomy of molar teeth	1	1
Aesthetic orthodontics	3	5
Cosmetic plastic surgery procedures		
Cosmetic plastic surgery (in general without specifying what)	4	11
Pinnaplasty	7	6

Procedure	Number of health authorities 1995/6 (n = 23)	Number of health authorities 1996/7 (n = 26)
Tattoo removal	9	8
Liposuction	7	6
Lipectomy	4	4
Abdominoplasty	5	4
Mastopexy	7	4
Breast augmentation	9	10
Breast reduction	3	4
Correction of inverted nipple	3	2
Buttock lift	5	4
Thigh lift	3	2
Arm lift	3	2
Surgery on ageing face	5	3
Blepharoplasty	6	5
Rhinoplasty	8	10
Repair of nipple	3	3
Reconstruction of breast	2	2
Prosthesis for breast	1	1
Other plastic operations on breast	1	1
Plastic excision of skin abdominal wall	1	2
Plastic excision of skin other sites	1	2
Removal adult birth marks	1	2
Insertion of penile prosthesis	1	0
Plastic excision skin of head or neck	0	1
Gastroplasty	0	1
Chelation therapy	2	2
Weight control/reduction surgery	1	3
Allergy assessment in environmentally controlled units	1	1
Benign non-genital warts	2	2
Circumcision other than religious reasons	3	3
Hyperbaric oxygen therapy except for decompression illness, early carbon dioxide poisoning and gas gangrene	1	1
Mass cholesterol screening for people at low risk	1	0
Pulse dye laser treatment	1	4
Bone density (as a population screening procedure)	2	2

Procedure	Number of health authorities 1995/6 (n = 23)	Number of health authorities 1996/7 (n = 26)
Radial keratotomy	1	1
Multi-allergy syndrome	1	1
Residential psychotherapy	0	2
Residential social treatment of drug or alcohol misuse	0	1
Long-term analytic psychotherapy	0	1
Cochlear implants	0	2
Sleep apnoea studies	0	2
Hospital or community clinic-base treatment for impotence	0	1
Vasectomy for under-25s	0	1
Sterilization for under-25s	0	1
Excimer laser surgery for short sight	0	2
Triple testing for Down's syndrome	0	1
Clinical ecology	0	1
Spinal computerized implants for chronic back pain	0	1
Psychotherapy	0	1
Counselling	0	1
Hysterectomy as treatment for dysfunctional uterine bleeding	0	1
Referrals and treatment for snoring which is not accompanied by sleep apnoea	0	1

REFERENCES

Aaron, Henry J. (1992). The Oregon experiment. In M. A. Strosberg *et al.* (eds) *Rationing America's Medical Care: the Oregon Plan and Beyond.* Washington, DC: The Brookings Institution.

Aaron, Henry J. and Schwartz, William B. (1984). *The Painful Prescription.* Washington, DC: The Brookings Institution.

Abel-Smith, Brian, Figueras, Josep, Holland, Walter, McKee, Martin and Mossialis, Elias (1995). *Choices in Health Policy: An Agenda for the European Union.* Aldershot: Dartmouth.

Appleby, John (1993). Data briefing: Steptoe and sons . . . and daughters. *Health Director,* 2, 13.

Association of County Councils/Association of Metropolitan Authorities (1995). *Who Gets Community Care?* London: ACC/AMA.

Audit Commission (1993). *Passing the Bucks: the Impact of Standard Spending Assessments on Economy, Efficiency and Effectiveness.* London: HMSO.

Audit Commission (1995a). *Local Authority Performance Indicators: Appendix to Volumes 1 and 2.* London: HMSO.

Audit Commission (1995b). *Briefing on GP Fundholding.* London: HMSO.

Baumol, William J. (1995). *Health Care as a Handicraft Industry.* London: The Office of Health Economics.

Beiner, Ronald (1983). *Political Judgment.* Chicago: University of Chicago Press.

Berlin, Isaiah (1991). The pursuit of the ideal. In Henry Hardy (ed.) *The Crooked Timber of Humanity.* New York: Alfred A. Knopf.

Bernstein, Steven J., Kosecoff, Jacqueline, Gray, David, Hampton, John R. and Brooke, Robert H. (1993). The appropriateness of the use of cardiovascular procedures. *International Journal of Technology Assessment in Health Care,* 9, 3–10.

Blustein, Jan and Marmor, Theodore R. (1992). Cutting waste by making rules: promises, pitfalls and realistic prospects. *University of Pennsylvania Law Review,* 140(5), 1543–72.

Bottomley, Virginia (1994). Rationing in action. Letter in *British Medical Journal*, 308(29), 338.

Bowie, Cameron, Richardson, Ann and Sykes, Wendy (1995). Consulting the public about health service priorities. *British Medical Journal*, 311, 1155–8.

Bowling, Ann (1993). *What People Say about Prioritising Health Services*. London: King's Fund Centre.

Braybrooke, David (1987). *Meeting Needs*. Princeton, NJ: Princeton University Press.

British Medical Association (1995). *Medical Ethics Today*. London: BMJ Publishing Group.

Browse, Sir Norman (1995). Evidence to the House of Commons Health Committee First Report Session 1994–95. In *Priority Setting in the NHS: Purchasing. Vol. II Minutes of Evidence*, HC 134-II, p. 72. London: HMSO.

Buchanan, James M. (1965). *The Inconsistencies of the National Health Service*. London: The Institute of Economic Affairs.

Cabases, Juan M. (1995). The guaranteed health care entitlement in Spain. Paper given at the Hard Choices in Health Care Conference, London, 21 November.

Calabresi, Guido and Bobbitt, Philip (1978). *Tragic Choices*. New York: Norton and Company.

Callahan, Daniel (1990). *What Kind of Life*. New York: Simon and Schuster.

Cambridge and Huntingdon Health Commission (1995). *Monthly Report on ECRs/Special Needs: Position as at 16 March 1995*. Cambridge: Cambridge and Huntingdon Health Commission Committee.

Carr-Hill, R., Hardman, G., Martin, S., Peacock, S., Sheldon, T. and Smith, P. (1994). *A Formula for Distributing NHS Revenues Based on Small Area Use of Hospital Beds*. York: Centre for Health Economics, University of York.

Carr-Hill, Roy (1995). Welcome? To the brave new world of evidence based medicine. *Social Science and Medicine*, 41(11), 1467–8.

Chadwick, Ruth (1993). Justice in priority setting. In Richard Smith (ed.) *Rationing in Action*. London: BMJ Publishing Group.

Challah, S., Wing, A. J., Bauer, R., Morris, R. W. and Schroeder, S. A. (1984). Negative selection of patients for dialysis and transplantation in the United Kingdom. *British Medical Journal*, 306, 1119–22.

Chancellor of the Exchequer (1995). *Financial Statement and Budget Report, 1996–97*. London: HMSO.

Chief Medical Officer of Health (1987). *On the State of the Public Health*. London: HMSO.

Cochrane, Murray, Ham, Chris, Henginbotham, Chris and Smith, Richard (1991). Rationing: at the cutting edge. *British Medical Journal*, 303, 1039–42.

Cooper, Michael H. (1975). *Rationing Health Care*. London: Croom Helm.

Craven, B. M., Steward, G. T. and Taghavi, M. (1994). Amateurs confronting specialists: expenditure on AIDS in England. *Journal of Public Policy*, 13(4), 305–25.

Crisp, Roger (1991). QALYs and the mentally handicapped. *Bulletin of Medical Ethics*, April, 13–16.

Cummings, Jacqueline (1994). Core services and priority-setting: the New Zealand experience. *Health Policy*, 29, 41–60.

Daniels, Norman (1992). Justice and health care rationing: Lessons from Oregon. In M. A. Strosberg *et al.* (eds) *Rationing America's Medical Care: the Oregon Plan and Beyond*. Washington, DC: The Brookings Institution.

Day, Patricia and Klein, Rudolf (1985). Central accountability and local decision making: towards a new NHS. *British Medical Journal*, 290, 1676–8.

Day, Patricia and Klein, Rudolf (1987). *Accountabilities*. London: Tavistock Publications.

de Kervasdoué, Jean, Kimberley, John R. and Rodwin, Victor G. (1984). *The End of an Illusion: The Future of Health Policy in Western Industrialized Nations*. Berkeley: University of California Press.

Department of Health and Social Security (1968). *NHS: Twentieth Anniversary Conference Report*. London: HMSO.

d'Iribarne, Philippe (1969). De politiques rationelles de santé et de sécurité. *Analyse et Prevision*, 8, 725–36.

Donaldson, Cam (1995). 'Economics, public health and health care purchasing: reinventing the wheel?' *Health Policy*, 33, 79–90.

Dowie, Jack and Elstein, Arthur (eds)(1988). *Professional Judgment: a Reader in Clinical Decision Making*. Cambridge: Cambridge University Press.

Doyal, L. and Gough, I. (1991). *A Theory of Human Need*. London: Macmillan.

Dunning, A. J. (1992). *Choices in Health Care*. Rijswijk, The Netherlands: Ministry of Welfare, Health and Cultural Affairs.

Eddy, David M. (1988). Variations in physician practice: the role of uncertainty. In J. Dowie and A. Elstein (eds) *Professional Judgment: a Reader in Clinical Decision Making*. Cambridge: Cambridge University Press.

Edgar, Wendy (1995). Health care priority setting in New Zealand. Paper given at the International Seminar on Healthcare Priority Setting, Birmingham, 18–19 March.

Effective Health Care (1992). *The Treatment of Persistent Glue Ear in Children*, No 4. Leeds: School of Public Health, University of Leeds.

Egan, Timothy (1991). Oregon shakes up pioneering health plan for the poor. *New York Times*, 22 February.

Elder, Andrew T. and Fox, Keith A. A. (1992). Thrombolytic treatment for elderly patients. *British Medical Journal*, 305, 846–7.

Elster, Jon (1992). *Local Justice: How Institutions Allocate Scarce Goods and Necessary Burdens*. Cambridge: Cambridge University Press.

Evans, Donald (1995). Infertility and the NHS. *British Medical Journal*, 311, 1586.

Fahey, T., Griffiths, S. and Peters, T. J. (1995). Evidence based purchasing: understanding results of clinical trials and systematic reviews. *British Medical Journal*, 311, 1056–9.

Farrow, Stephen and Jewell, David (1993). Opening the gate: referrals from primary to secondary care. In S. Frankel and R. West (eds) *Rationing and Rationality in the National Health Service*. London: Macmillan.

Feest, T. G., Mistry, C. D., Grimes, S. S. and Mallick, N. P. (1990). Incidence of advanced chronic renal failure and the need for end stage renal replacement treatment. *British Medical Journal*, 301, 897–900.

Fishkin, James S. (1991). *Democracy and Deliberation*. New Haven, CT: Yale University Press.

Fox, Daniel M. (1993). *Power and Illness*. Berkeley: University of California Press.

Fox, Daniel M. and Leichter, Howard M. (1991). Rationing care in Oregon: the new accountability. *Health Affairs*, Summer, 7–26.

Frankel, Stephen and West, Robert (eds) (1993). *Rationing and Rationality in the National Health Service: the Persistence of Waiting Lists*. London: Macmillan.

Freidson, Eliot (1971). *Profession of Medicine*. New York: Dodd, Mead & Company.

Fuchs, Victor R. (1974). *Who Shall Live?* New York: Basic Books.

Garland, Michael J. (1992). Rationing in public: Oregon's priority-setting methodology. In M. A. Strosberg *et al.* (eds) *Rationing America's Medical Care: the Oregon Plan and Beyond*. Washington, DC: The Brookings Institution.

General Medical Council (1995). *Good Medical Practice*. London: GMC.

Glennerster, Howard (1975). *Social Services Budgets and Social Policy*. London: Allen & Unwin.

Grimley Evans, J. (1993). Health care rationing and elderly people. In Michael Tunbridge (ed.) *Rationing of Health Care in Medicine*. London: Royal College of Physicians.

Guillebaud, C. W. (chairman) (1956). *Report of the Committee of Enquiry into the Cost of the National Health Service*. London: HMSO.

Hadorn, David C. (1991). Setting health care priorities in Oregon. *Journal of the American Medical Association*, 265, 2218–25.

Halper, Thomas (1989). *The Misfortunes of Others: End-stage Renal Disease in the United Kingdom*. Cambridge: Cambridge University Press.

Ham, Chris (ed.) (1988). *Health Care Variations*. London: King's Fund Institute.

Ham, Chris (1995). What can we learn from international experience. In R.

J. Maxwell (ed.) *Rationing Health Care*. Edinburgh: Churchill Livingstone.

Ham, Chris, Honigsbaum, Frank and Thompson, David (1993). *Priority Setting for Health Gain*. Birmingham: Health Services Management Centre, University of Birmingham.

Harris, John (1988). EQALYTY. In Peter Byrne (ed.) *Health Rights and Resources*. London: King Edward's Hospital Fund for London.

Harris, Ralph and Seldon, Arthur (1979). *Over-ruled on Welfare*. London: The Institute of Economic Affairs.

Harrison, Stephen (1995). A policy agenda for health care rationing. In R. J. Maxwell (ed.) *Rationing Health Care*. Edinburgh: Churchill Livingstone.

Harrison, Stephen and Hunter, David J. (1994). *Rationing Health Care*. London: Institute for Public Policy Research.

Harvey, Ian (1993). And so to bed: access to inpatient services. In S. Frankel and R. West (eds) *Rationing and Rationality in the National Health Service*. London: Macmillan.

Health Committee of the House of Commons (1995). *Priority Setting in the NHS: Purchasing*. Fifth Report, Session 1994–5. London: HMSO.

Heginbotham, Chris (1992). Jam tomorrow? *Health Service Journal*, 5 (March), 24–25.

Heginbotham, Christopher (1993). Healthcare priority setting: a survey of doctors, managers and the general public. In R. Smith (ed.) *Rationing in Action*. London: BMJ Publishing Group.

Hennessy, Peter (1993). *Never Again: Britain 1945–1951*. London: Vintage.

Hill, Michael J. (1972). *The Sociology of Public Administration*. London: Weidenfeld and Nicolson.

Hills, John (1990). *The State of Welfare*. Oxford: Clarendon Press.

Hoffenberg, Sir Raymond (1987). *Clinical Freedom*. London: The Nuffield Provincial Hospitals Trust.

Hopkins, Anthony (1995). Some reservations about clinical guidelines. *Archives of Disease in Childhood*, 72, 70–5.

Huby, Meg and Dix, Gill (1992). *Evaluating the Social Fund*. Department of Social Security Research Report No. 9. London: HMSO.

Hunter, David (1991). Pain of going public. *The Health Service Journal*, 29 August, 20.

Hunter, David (1993). *Rationing Dilemmas in Healthcare*. Birmingham: National Association of Health Authorities and Trusts.

Hunter, Kathryn Montgomery (1991). *Doctors' Stories: the Narrative Structure of Medical Knowledge*. Princeton, NJ: Princeton University Press.

Institute of Housing (1990). *Housing Allocations: Report of a Survey of Local Authorities in England and Wales*. Coventry: Institute of Housing.

Jacobson, Bobbie (1994). Translating research into practice – from rhetoric to reality. In E. Gilman, S. Murray, L. Somervaille and R. Strachan (eds) *Resource Allocation and Health Needs: from Research to Policy.* London: HMSO.

Jenkins, Simon (1995a). *Accountable to None.* London: Hamish Hamilton.

Jenkins, Simon (1995b). Life and death is not for lawyers. *The Times*, 11 March.

Jenkins, Simon (chairman) (1995c). *Taking Charge: the Rebirth of Local Democracy.* The Final Report of the Commission for Local Democracy. London: Municipal Journal Books.

Jennett, Bryan (1986). *High Technology Medicine: Benefits and Burdens.* Oxford: Oxford University Press.

Jonsen, Albert R. (1986). Bentham in a box: technology assessment and health care allocation. *Law, Medicine and Health Care*, 14(3–4), 172–4.

Judge, Ken (1978). *Rationing Social Services.* London: Heinemann.

Kaplan, Robert M. (1992). A quality-of-life approach to health resource allocation. In M. A. Strosberg *et al.* (eds) *Rationing America's Medical Care: the Oregon Plan and Beyond.* Washington, DC: The Brookings Institution.

Kingman, Sharon (1996). Renal services in UK are underfunded, says report. *British Medical Journal*, 312, 267.

Kitzhaber, J. and Kenny, A. M. (1995). On the Oregon trail. In R. J. Maxwell (ed.) *Rationing Health Care.* Edinburgh: Churchill Livingstone.

Klein, Rudolf (1975). Introduction. In R. Klein (ed.) *Inflation and Priorities.* London: Centre for Studies in Social Policy.

Klein, Rudolf (1991). On the Oregon trail: rationing health care. *British Medical Journal*, 302, 1–2.

Klein, Rudolf (1994). Can we restrict the health care menu? *Health Policy*, 27, 103–12.

Klein, Rudolf (1995). *The New Politics of the NHS.* London: Longman.

Klein, Rudolf (1996). The NHS and the new scientism: solution or delusion? *Quarterly Journal of Medicine*, 89, 85–7.

Klein, Rudolf and O'Higgins, Michael (1985). Social policy after incrementalism. In Rudolf Klein and Michael O'Higgins (eds) *The Future of Welfare.* Oxford: Blackwell.

Klein, Rudolf and Redmayne, Sharon (1992). *Patterns of Priorities: a Study of the Purchasing and Rationing Policies of Health Authorities.* Birmingham: National Association of Health Authorities and Trusts Research Paper No. 7.

Klein, Rudolf, Day, Patricia and Redmayne, Sharon (1995). Memorandum. In House of Commons Health Committee First Report Session 1994–95 *Priority Setting in the NHS: Purchasing. Vol. II Minutes of Evidence*, HC 134-II, pp. 1–5. London: HMSO.

Lack, Alistair and Fletcher, Sarajane (1993). 'Surgical waiting lists analysis', unpublished paper. Salisbury: Salisbury Hospital Mimeo.

Lapsley, Helen (chair) (1995). *Guidelines for the Development and*

Implementation of Clinical Guidelines. Report of the Quality of Care and Health Outcomes Committee. Canberra: Australian Government Publishing Service.

Lenaghan, Joanne (1995). Developing a national framework of entitlements. Paper presented at the Hard Choices in Health Care Conference, London, 21 November.

Lee, Tim (1996). *The Search for Equity*. Aldershot: Avebury.

Lipsky, Michael (1980). *Street-level Bureaucracy*. New York: Russell Sage Foundation.

Logan, R. F. L., Ashley, J. S. A., Klein, R. E. and Robin, D. M. (1972). *Dynamics of Medical Care*. London: London School of Hygiene and Tropical Medicine, Memoir No. 14.

Longley, Diane (1993). *Public Law and Health Service Accountability*. Buckingham: Open University Press.

McKee, Martin and Clarke, Aileen (1995). Guidelines, enthusiasms, uncertainty and the limits to purchasing. *British Medical Journal*, 310, 101–4.

McPherson, Klim (1994). How should health policy be modified by the evidence of medical practice variations? In M. Marinker (ed.) *Controversies in Health Care Policies*. London: BMJ Publishing Group.

Mamode, Nizam (1993). Denying access more costly. Letter in *British Medical Journal*, 306, 1408.

Marmor, Theodore R. (1983). *Political Analysis and American Health Care*. Cambridge: Cambridge University Press.

Marmor, Theodore R. (1994). *Understanding Health Care Reform*. New Haven, CT: Yale University Press.

Martin, J. R. (1984). *Hospitals in Trouble*. Oxford: Basil Blackwell.

Maxwell, Robert J. (ed.) (1995). *Rationing Health Care*. British Medical Bulletin, Vol. 51. Edinburgh: Churchill Livingstone.

Maynard, A. and Ludbrook, A. (1980). Budget allocation in the National Health Service. *Journal of Social Policy*, 9, 289–312.

Maynard, Alan (1994). Prioritising health care – dreams and reality'. In M. Malek (ed.) *Setting Priorities in Health Care*. Chichester: John Wiley & Sons.

Maynard, A. and Bloor, K. (1995). Help or hindrance? The role of economics in rationing health care. In R. J. Maxwell (ed.) *Rationing Health Care*. Edinburgh: Churchill Livingstone.

Mays, Nicholas (1995). Geographical resource allocation in the English National Health Service, 1971–1994. *International Journal of Epidemiology*, 24 (supplement 1), S96-S102.

Mechanic, David (1979). *Future Issues in Health Care: Social Policy and the Rationing of Medical Services*. New York: The Free Press.

Mechanic, David (1992). Professional judgment and the rationing of medical care. *University of Pennsylvania Law Review*, 140, 1713–54.

Mechanic, David (1995). Dilemmas in rationing health care services: the case for implicit rationing. *British Medical Journal*, 310, 1655–9.

Merrison, Sir Alec (chairman) (1979). *Report of the Royal Commission on the National Health Service*. London: HMSO.

Miller, Frances H. (1992). Denial of health care and informed consent in English and American law. *American Journal of Law and Medicine*, 18 (1/2), 37–71.

Minister of Health (1950). *National Health Service (England and Wales). Control of Expenditure: Memorandum by the Minister of Health*. London: Public Record Office (CAB 129/38).

Moynihan, Daniel Patrick (1996). Congress builds a coffin. *The New York Review of Books*, 43 (1), 33–6.

National Advisory Committee on Core Health and Disability Services (1994). *Third Report: Core Services for 1995/96*. Wellington, New Zealand: Core Services Committee.

NHS Executive (1995). *Priorities and Planning Guidance for the NHS: 1996/97*. Leeds: NHS Executive.

NHS Executive (1996). *Promoting Clinical Effectiveness: a Framework for Action in and Through the NHS*. Leeds: NHS Executive.

NHS Management Executive (1991). *Priorities and Planning Guidance for the NHS for 1992/93*. London: Department of Health (EL(91) 103).

NHS Management Executive (1992). *Priorities and Planning Guidance 1993/94*. London: Department of Health (EL(92)47).

NHS Management Executive (1993). *Priorities and Planning Guidance 1994–95*. Leeds: Department of Health (EL(93)54).

NHS Management Executive (1994). *Priorities and Planning Guidance for the NHS: 1995/96*. Leeds: NHS Management Executive.

Norheim, Ole Frithjof (1992). The guidelines for priority-setting in the Norwegian health care system. Paper presented at the European Society for Philosophy of Medicine and Health Care, 12–14 August, Budapest.

Ontario Ministry of Health (1994). *News Release: Grier Accepts Pringle Report*. Ottawa: Ministry of Health.

Organization for Economic Co-operation and Development (1994). *The Reform of Health Care Systems: a Review of Seventeen OECD countries*. Paris: OECD.

Parker, Roy (1975). Social administration and scarcity. In E. Butterworth and R. Holman (eds) *Social Welfare in Modern Britain*. London: Fontana.

Parliamentary Debates (1995). Vol. 267, No. 3, 17 November, cols 240–309.

Parsons, V. and Lock, P. M. (1980). Triage and the patient with renal failure. *Journal of Medical Ethics*, 6, 173–6.

Peacock, Stuart and Smith, Peter (1995). *The Resource Allocation Consequences of the New NHS Needs Formula*. York: Centre for Health Economics, University of York.

Pollock, Allyson M. (1995). The politics of destruction: rationing in the UK health care market. *Health Care Analysis*, 3 (4), 299–308.

Powell, J. Enoch (1966). *Medicine and Politics*. London: Pitman Medical.

Rae, Douglas (1981). *Equalities*. Cambridge, MA: Harvard University Press.

Rawls, John (1972). *A Theory of Justice*. Oxford: Oxford University Press.

Redmayne, Sharon (1995). *Reshaping the NHS: Strategies, Priorities and Resource Allocation*. Birmingham: National Association of Health Authorities and Trusts, Research Paper No. 16.

Redmayne, Sharon (1996). *Small Steps, Big Goals*. Birmingham: National Association of Health Authorities and Trusts.

Redmayne, Sharon and Klein, Rudolf (1993). Rationing in practice: the case of in vitro fertilisation. *British Medical Journal*, 306, 1521–4.

Redmayne, Sharon, Klein, Rudolf and Day, Patricia (1993). *Sharing out Resources: Purchasing and Priority Setting in the NHS*. Birmingham: National Association of Health Authorities and Trusts, Research Paper No. 11.

Resource Allocation Working Party (1976). *Sharing Resources for Health in England*. London: HMSO.

Richardson, Andrew, Charny, Mark and Hanmer-Lloyd, Stuart (1992). Public opinion and purchasing. *British Medical Journal*, 304, 680–2.

Roberts, Colin (1995). Rationing is a desperate measure. *Health Service Journal*, 12 January, 15.

Robinson, Ray (1993). Cost–benefit analysis. *British Medical Journal*, 307, 924–6.

Royal College of Obstetricians and Gynaecologists (1992). *Infertility: Guidance for Practice*. London: RCOG Press.

Royal College of Physicians (1995). *Setting Priorities in the NHS*. London: Royal College of Physicians.

Royal Courts of Justice (1995). *Regina* v. *Cambridge Health Authority ex parte 'B': Judgment*. London: Official Shorthand Writers to the Court.

Russell, Louise B. (1994). *Educated Guesses*. Berkeley: University of California Press.

Saper, Rupert and Laing, William (1995). Age of uncertainty. *Health Service Journal*, 26 October, 22–3.

Saunders, Kate (1995). How much is your child's life worth? *The Sunday Times*, 12 March.

Scrivens, Ellie (1979). Towards a theory of rationing. *Social Policy and Administration*, 13 (1), 53–64.

Secretary of State for Health (1989). *Working for Patients*. London: HMSO.

Secretary of State for Health (1991). *The Patient's Charter*. London: Department of Health.

Secretary of State for Health (1992a). *Department of Health and Office of Population Censuses and Surveys: Departmental Report*. London: HMSO.

Secretary of State for Health (1992b). *The Health of the Nation*. London: HMSO.

Secretary of State for Health (1993). *One Year On . . . a report on the Progress of the Health of the Nation*. London: HMSO.

Secretary of State for Health (1995). *Government Response to the First Report from the Health Committee Session 1994–95*. London: HMSO.

Secretary of State for Social Services (1976). *Priorities for Health and Personal Social Services in England*. London: HMSO.

Secretary of State for Social Services (1977). *The Way Forward*. London: HMSO.

Secretary of State for Social Services (1981). *Care in Action: a Handbook of Policies and Priorities for the Health and Personal Social Services in England*. London: HMSO.

Sheldon, Trevor A. (1992). Discounting health care decision-making: time for a change? *Journal of Public Health Medicine*, 14 (3), 250–6.

Smith, Richard (1991a). Where is the wisdom . . . ? The poverty of medical evidence. *British Medical Journal*, 303, 798–9.

Smith, Richard (1991b). Rationing: the search for sunlight. *British Medical Journal*, 303, 1561–2.

Smith, Richard (ed.) (1993). *Rationing in Action*. London: BMJ Publishing Group.

Spicker, Paul (1983). *The Allocation of Council Housing*. London: Shelter.

Spiegelhalter, D. J., Gore, S. M., Fitzpatrick, R., Fletcher, A. E., Jones, D. R. and Ox, D. R. (1992). Quality of life measures in health care III: resource allocation. *British Medical Journal*, 305, 1205–9.

Stevens, Andrew and Gabbay, John (1991). Needs assessment needs assessment. *Health Trends*, 23 (1), 20–3.

Strosberg, Martin A., Wiener, Joshua M., Baker, Robert and Fein, I. Alan (eds) (1992). *Rationing America's Medical Care: the Oregon Plan and Beyond*. Washington, DC: The Brookings Institution.

Surender, Rebecca, Bradlow, Jean, Coulter, Angela, Doll, Helen and Stewart Brown, Sarah (1995). Prospective study of trends in referral patterns in fundholding and non-fundholding practices in the Oxford region, 1990–4. *British Medical Journal*, 311, 1205–8.

Swedish Parliamentary Priorities Commission (1995). *Priorities in Health Care: Ethics, Economy, Implementation*. Stockholm: Regeringskansliets.

Thwaites, Sir Brian (1987). *The NHS: the End of the Rainbow?* Southampton: The Institute of Health Policy Studies, University of Southampton.

Toynbee, Polly (1995). Did the NHS cheat Jaymee? *The Independent*, 27 October.

Underwood, M. J. and Bailey, J. S. (1993). Coronary bypass surgery should not be offered to smokers. *British Medical Journal*, 306, 1047–8.

Veatch, Robert M. (1992). The Oregon experiment: needless and real worries. In M. A. Strosberg *et al.* (eds) *Rationing America's Medical Care: the Oregon Plan and Beyond*. Washington, DC: The Brookings Institution.

Walley, T. and Barton, S. (1995). A purchaser perspective of managing new drugs: interferon beta as a case study. *British Medical Journal*, 311, 796–9.

Walker, Robert, Dix, Gill and Huby, Meg, with the assistance of Anne Corden and Marilyn Thirlway (1992). *Working the Social Fund*. Department of Social Security Research Report No. 8 London: HMSO.

Weale, Albert (1979). Statistical lives and the principle of maximum benefit. *Journal of Medical Ethics*, 5, 185–95.

Weale, Albert (1990). The allocation of scarce medical resources: a democrat's dilemma. In Peter Byrne (ed.) *Medicine, Medical Ethics and the Value of Life*. Chichester: John Wiley & Sons.

Weale, Albert (1995). The ethics of rationing. In R. J. Maxwell (ed.) *Rationing Health Care*. Edinburgh: Churchill Livingstone.

Webster, Charles (1988). *The Health Service Since the War*. Vol. 1: *The NHS before 1957*. London: HMSO.

West, Robert (1993). Joining the queue: demand and decision-making. In S. Frankel and R. West (eds) *Rationing and Rationality in the National Health Service*. London: Macmillan.

Wildavsky, Aaron (1975). *Doing Better and Feeling Worse: the Political Pathology of Health Policy*. Berkeley: Graduate School of Public Policy, University of California Working Paper No. 19.

Wiles, R. and Patel, H. (1995). *Report of the Third National Survey of NHS Funding of Fertility Services*. London: Royal College of Health.

Williams, Alan (1992). Cost-effectiveness analysis: is it ethical? *Journal of Medical Ethics*, 18, 7–11.

Willigenburg, Theo van (1993). Communitarian illusions: or why the Dutch proposal for setting priorities in health care must fail. *Health Care Analysis*, 1, 49–52.

Wing, A. J. (1990). Can we meet the real need for dialysis and transplantation? *British Medical Journal*, 301, 885–6.

Zimmern, Ron (1995). Insufficient to simply be efficient. *Health Service Journal*, 24 (August), 19.

INDEX

THE INCOMPETENT DOCTOR
BEHIND CLOSED DOORS

Marilynn M. Rosenthal

Based on qualitative, ethnographic research carried out in England and Sweden, this book examines a neglected area of professional self-regulation. It explores the range of informal and quasi-formal mechanisms used by doctor colleagues, health care managers and professional organizations in attempts to cope with the 'problem' or 'incompetent' doctor. Focused on Consultant Surgeons and senior General Practitioners, extensive interviews reveal a repertoire of mechanisms that include, amongst others, the 'Frank Talk', 'Protective Support', the 'Veiled Threat', being 'Forced out of the Partnership', the attempted 'Golden Handshake' and, when all else fails, 'Stalemate and Marginalization'. Each chapter includes a number of specific cases as well as extensive quotations from those interviewed. How information is gathered and assessed, the relative success or failure of these mechanisms, the factors that determine their use or non-use, medical perceptions of mistakes and the changing attitudes of the public are examined.

The book includes a discussion of current changes in the National Health Service and their likely impact on these issues and quality assurance in medical care. Some comparisons with the informal processes in Sweden provide insight into the universality of the informal mechanisms. The book ends with a proposal for a total, integrated peer review system that recognizes and strengthens the informal mechanisms and links them to systematic clinical practice analysis and other efforts that enhance the medical profession's commitment to effective self-regulation.

> Professor Rosenthal has done her job extremely well. In an area in which there are few facts and figures, and those that exist are largely held in secrecy, she has produced a clear picture of what actually is going on and we should be grateful to her.
>
> Sir Raymond Hoffenberg

Contents
The issues: why they are important – Making mistakes: how doctors think about this – Friendly efforts: the informal mechanisms – Frustration mounts: requiring 'the skill of a politician and the tact of a diplomat' – Behind closed doors: how effective are the informal mechanisms? – Empirical research on medical mishaps and mistakes: challenges to professional norms – Coming changes: will they make a difference? – References and notes – Index.

192 pp   0 335 19506 7 (Paperback)   0 335 19507 5 (Hardback)

ACCREDITATION
PROTECTING THE PROFESSIONAL OR THE CONSUMER?

Ellie Scrivens

Politicians are worried whether health services are providing value for money. Members of the public worry whether they will be able to receive the health care they need, when they need it. We all worry that the health services that treat us when we are ill might be causing more harm than good. In the United States, Australia and Canada most hospitals and other health services are scrutinized by professional peers to establish adherence to good practice, in a system known as accreditation. Why have accreditation systems developed, what form do they take, what issues do they raise, and how useful are they in achieving the goals of health services to provide better care? This book examines these questions and explains the policy and the practical issues in establishing such systems. It will be of interest to a wide range of health professionals as well as students of health policy and health services management.

Contents
Introduction – Part 1: The history and structure of accreditation systems – The essence of accreditation – The United Kingdom experience – The accreditation experience – Part 2: Issues in the design and implementation of accreditation systems – Standards Design and measurement – The organization of accreditation systems – Part 3: Policy and accreditation – The policy implications of accreditation – The future – References – Select bibliography – Index.

200 pp   0 335 19491 5 (Paperback)   0 335 19492 3 (Hardback)

IMPLEMENTING PLANNED MARKETS IN HEALTH CARE
BALANCING SOCIAL AND ECONOMIC RESPONSIBILITY
Richard B. Saltman and Casten von Otter (eds)

- What lessons can be learned from the health reform process to date?
- What direction will future health reforms take in the industrialized world?

Implementing Planned Markets in Health Care brings together an international team of experts to address these important questions. Drawing on experiences in Northern Europe and the United States, it examines the key concepts behind the present push towards health reform in the industrialized world:

- contracting and solidarity
- contestable v. competitive markets
- the role of vouchers
- physicians' clinical autonomy

Also included are case studies of planned market approaches based on contracts, patient choice, and on quality of care. The book concludes with a broad comparative assessment of the main themes and points towards the most likely developments in future *planned market* models of health care.

Contents
Introduction – Part 1: The politics of contracting – Contracting and the purchaser–provider split – Contracting and solidarity – Regulation of planned markets in health care – Contracting and political boards in planned markets – Part 2: Balancing incentives and accountability – Costs, productivity and financial outcomes of managed care – Vouchers in planned markets – Clinical autonomy and planned markets – Part 3: Constructing entrepreneurial providers – Self-governing trusts and GP fundholders – Implementing planned markets in health services – Competitive hospital markets based on quality – Part 4: Conclusion – Index.

Contributors
Anders Anell, Göran Arvidsson, Mats Brommels, Aad A. de Roo, Stephen Harrison, Nancy M. Kane, Christian M. Koeck, Julian Le Grand, Britta Neugaard, Ray Robinson, Richard B. Saltman, Clive H. Smee, Casten von Otter.

272 pp   0 335 19425 7 (Paperback)   0 335 19426 5 (Hardback)

Learning Resources
Centre